Beginning to Write

Writing activities for elementary and intermediate learners

*Arthur Brookes and
Peter Grundy*

CAMBRIDGE
UNIVERSITY PRESS

PUBLISHED BY THE PRESS SYNDICATE OF THE UNIVERSITY OF CAMBRIDGE
The Pitt Building, Trumpington Street, Cambridge, United Kingdom

CAMBRIDGE UNIVERSITY PRESS
The Edinburgh Building, Cambridge CB2 2RU, UK
40 West 20th Street, New York, NY 10011–4211, USA
477 Williamstown Road, Port Melbourne, VIC 3207, Australia
Ruiz de Alarcón 13, 28014 Madrid, Spain
Dock House, The Waterfront, Cape Town 8001, South Africa

http://www.cambridge.org

First published 1998
Fifth printing 2003

Printed in the United Kingdom at the University Press, Cambridge

Typeset in Sabon 10.5/12

A catalogue record for this book is available from the British Library

Library of Congress Cataloguing in Publication data
Brookes, Arthur.
    Beginning to write : writing activities for elementary and intermediate
learners / Arthur Brookes and Peter Grundy.
    p.   cm. – (Cambridge handbooks for language teachers)
    Includes bibliographical references (p.) and index.
    ISBN 0-521-58979-7 (pbk.)
    1. English language – Composition and exercises – Study and teaching
(Elementary)   I. Grundy, Peter.   II. Title.   III. Series.
LB 1576.B764   1998
372.62'3–dc21   '2

ISBN 0 521 58979 7 paperback

Contents

Contents

Contents

Acknowledgements

The authors and publishers are grateful to the authors, publishers and others who have given permission for the use of copyright material identified in the text. It has not been possible to identify the sources of all the material used and in such cases the publishers would welcome information from copyright owners.

Mistletoe Pizzeria for the handbill on p. 53; Boots Opticians for the extract on contact lenses on p. 72; British Telecom for the extract on malicious calls on p. 72; The Met. Office for the material on p. 76 © Crown copyright. Reproduced with the permission of the controller of HMSO.

Read this first

We have written this book because we believe that it is important to teach writing as a skill in its own right from an early stage in language learning. The majority of the exercises in this book are concerned with this kind of writing.

The introduction which follows examines what writing is and how it should be taught. It concludes with a section providing advice on how to use the hundred or so activities which you will find in this book.

The activities in this book are suitable for elementary or intermediate learners of all ages. They are grouped in chapters to help you find the kind of activity you are looking for more easily. The activities in the early chapters are, on the whole, easier, and involve students in copying-type exercises which help to build confidence, including some which are equally enjoyable ways of using writing as a support for language learning. Later groups of activities are, on the whole, more difficult. Some give practice at writing completed products, while others concentrate on a single aspect of the writing process. There are also activities on the use of computers in teaching writing (though many of these exercises can also be used without them). Finally, there are activities on assessment – especially the learners' own self-assessment.

We often suggest that students should work in pairs or groups. There are two reasons for this. The first is to raise the students' awareness of the writing process by planning their work in the particularly conscious way that writing collaboratively involves. The second is to make writing a less lonely or secretive activity than it sometimes appears to be.

You will also notice that we rarely want writing lessons to result in products for the teacher to assess. Instead, we often suggest making a wall display of student writing – this way, writing is taken seriously, readership is provided, and students learn from each other. At other times, writing triggers further writing or discussion. This approach should make your work easier and should make writing less stressful for your students. It also provides a more public, genuine context for writing.

The authors of every book owe a lot to others. In our case we recognise the influence of those whose work has caused us all to rethink the teaching of writing in recent years, not only basic researchers, but particularly also practitioner-researchers. Of these, we especially recommend Raimes (1987) as a stimulating general book, Hedge (1988) as a classroom-based book, and White (1988) for an excellent chapter-long discussion of general issues. We have also learnt a lot from our own students, both practising teachers on MA courses, and EAP and general language learners. For years we have been trying out the ideas they inspired in us – and now we are passing these on to you as a book.

However we would not be passing these ideas on to you in such an orderly way were it not for our editor, Penny Ur, who together with Alison Sharpe at CUP helped us first to focus our original ideas more precisely and then greatly to improve the earlier drafts of the book itself. We are also very grateful to Jane Clifford at CUP who looked after the book from beginning to end, and to Liz Driscoll whose meticulous editing saved us many embarrassments.

Finally, thank you for reading our book. We are genuinely interested in how it works for you, and hope that you won't hesitate to write to us with any thoughts or reactions you may have.

Introduction

All of us who are practising teachers will be aware that the skill of writing well in a second language is important and needs separate and special attention. Writing is, of course, not easy, but it is less difficult than many students and their teachers imagine. The 100 or so activities that follow this introduction give you the opportunity to try for yourselves those that you think will best suit you and your students.

However, you will understand the purpose of these activities better and, furthermore, be able to adapt them and even invent new activities of your own by taking a step back from the classroom and looking at the nature of writing itself and what others have thought about it. A discussion of this topic comes next in the Introduction and is followed by suggestions as to how it is possible to apply these writing principles in the classroom. The last part of the Introduction gives you advice about how to put the activities into practice.

1 The nature of writing

The study of language in the twentieth century has tended to concentrate on spoken language. Written language was thought by some to be spoken language put into written form. Many linguists from de Saussure through to Chomsky, for what seemed like good reasons at the time, neglected the written mode in favour of the spoken. This, however, contributed to the fact that writing was for a long time a neglected area in language teaching. Furthermore, the assumption that writing is putting the spoken language into written form is only true for activities like taking down dictation or transcribing a tape.

Differences between writing and speaking

There are many differences, big and small, between writing and speaking.

a Writing is more 'attended to' than speech, i.e. we are more conscious of what we are doing and tend to attach more importance to correctness of every kind, knowing that our reader can return to our writing but we cannot, and that we cannot easily rectify mis-understandings on the part of the reader.

b Writing has text-types of its own, different from those of speech; an example that comes readily to mind is that the way we arrange what we have to say in telephone or face-to-face conversations is different from the arrangement of material in letters or e-mail messages.

c Writing can make use of visual devices in a way which speech cannot, as in the following advertisement for underwear for large men:

> # H U R R Y ! ! !
>
> *while stocks last*
> *Why not order our*
>
> **X** – **tra large**
> **Y** – **fronts**
> **Z** – **ebra patterned**

Together with the chosen script, such visual devices can be compared with the different effects and meanings in spoken English produced by, for instance, different stress and intonation patterns. When we write, not all of us use script consistently, correctly, and effectively!

d Writing-systems may assist groups of people to communicate, as in the case of Chinese where the different 'dialects' are mutually unin-telligible in spoken form but share a common written form; the position is reversed in the case of Hindi and Urdu where the different written forms make it difficult for the speakers of those rather simi-lar spoken languages to communicate in writing. The script used in different writing-systems is of great importance. It takes many years of careful study to master the classic Chinese writing-system. Even simple alphabetic-systems such as that used for English have many features and potentialities that need to be consciously learnt.

e The spelling-systems of almost all languages that use alphabetic writing-systems are based to some extent on how the word is spoken, but only partly so: we can often trace not only the history of words including from which language they have been borrowed, but also their relation to each other in spite of differences in pronunciation – examples taken from English are *anxious, anxiety*; *receipt, reception*; and the grammatical endings of *loved, kissed,* and *hated*.

f Because, as we noted above, writing is more attended to than speech, we set higher and higher standards for ourselves as we get better at it;

so while listening, speaking and reading all feel easier as we become more proficient, the better we get at writing the easier it is to please others, but the harder to please ourselves.

g Up to now, there have been more varieties of acceptable spoken than written English used internationally. Written English has so far been more uniform, except for relatively minor issues such as the differences between British and American spelling. Individual writers are, of course, expected to be consistent in their use of one or the other. However, it is not yet fully clear what the effect of the widespread use of English for e-mail and on the Internet will eventually be.

The purpose of writing

If we ask ourselves why we write at all, the answer may well be to get information to someone we can't presently talk to. Thus writing allows us to transcend time (when we leave a note for someone to pick up later) or space (when we send a letter through the post). A second answer might be (especially when we think of the needs of society as a whole) to solve the problem of volume, of having to store more than the human brain can remember. A less likely, but nevertheless important, third reason for writing might be to filter and shape our experience. Below we elaborate briefly on each of these reasons and ask you to think of them in relation to your students.

Transcending the here and now

When someone in Japan and someone in Europe want to communicate, their working hours overlap barely if at all, so that even the telephone will be less useful than letters, faxes and e-mail messages. Or a headteacher busy in the office and needing to communicate with a member of staff may send a message in the form of a written note. In each of these cases, writing transcends space. But it can also transcend time. So our desk drawers, filing cabinets and computer hard disks are full of previously recorded written information that we think we may need at some time in the future.

Task

Focus on an individual learner in your class. Think of two or three real-world needs that your learner might have to communicate in writing with people not present in the here and now.

The problem of volume

From the beginning of history, man has found it useful to be able to store information reliably, first using specially trained 'memorisers' from within the community, and then moving on to developing writing-systems. This is especially true of modern industrialised society where the sheer volume of information means that there is too much to recall. The written form is the most convenient for this purpose, because though we now have facilities for storing spoken material, it is much harder to access or to skim through than written material. Thus at school, writing is a skill we must learn in order to become full and useful members of society. This is, of course, also true in our own personal lives. For instance, most of us keep an address book with the names, addresses and telephone numbers of people we may wish to contact at some time in the future, as we cannot remember them all. And the increasingly large amount of information stored on computer is itself almost always inputted and accessed as written text.

Task

Think of the very last class you taught. Almost inevitably, your students will have written down something you or they wanted to keep for subsequent use which they knew they would not other-wise be able to recall. Spend a moment thinking about how this was done, and how and when it will be referred to in the future.

Filtering and shaping experience

You cannot write without filtering information: as we write, we think about what to write and how to represent our experience. Indeed, we may well find that writing helps us to come to terms with our experience and understand it better. When we edit what we have written, our writing itself goes through a further filter. The result is that our writing provides our readers with a condensed, economical, carefully considered version of what we might say to them which is very different from spoken forms. In a sense, we have clarified what we think by forcing ourselves to write it down.

As well as filtering, we compose. That is, we consider how to present what we want to communicate – with what purpose, for which reader(s), and in what order. For instance, if someone sends us a present, we must decide whether to thank them in writing or not, and if in writing, whether to write a brief message on a card or a slightly longer letter on writing paper.

Task

Think of the very last writing task you gave your students. To what extent did you explicitly set aside time for the students to decide how to compose the text, even if it was very brief and designed to be read only by their partners?

The uses to which writing is put in the real world

We have found it helpful, as we are sure you will, when devising writing tasks for the classroom, to discover first the real-world writing our students do outside the English classroom in both their first and second language. This can then be used to extend the range and relevance of their classroom writing tasks. Before you read the list that follows, try the following task.

Task

Make a list of the different uses to which you have put your writing skills in the past week in both your first and second language. When you have done this, compare your list with the list produced by a class of native-speaker second-year University students training to be teachers which you will find on the next page.

On the next page is a list of real-world writing purposes drawn up by twenty second-year English native-speaker University students training to be teachers. The students were asked to list all the different uses to which they had put their writing skills during the previous week. The 62-item list is divided into two columns. The first column lists uses mentioned by two or more students, the number of students being indicated in parenthesis after each item. The second column lists single mentions.

You may well be surprised at the length and variety of the list. Note that it contains a range of categories, including functional writing (reports), place where the writing occurs (the blackboard), private writing (love letters), public writing (notices), lengthy writing (seminar papers), shorter pieces (greetings cards), copying or dictation (recipes), writing that everyone does in literate societies (writing down an address), writing that only some people ever do (applying for an overdraft), highly specialised writing (writing a horoscope), creative writing (songs), and intellectually demanding writing (doing crosswords).

Making a shopping list (10)
Writing a formal letter (10)
Making notes in a diary (10)
Writing letters to friends (9)
Writing an essay (9)
Writing greetings cards (8)
Making notes for the family (7)
Taking lecture notes (7)
Signing a cheque (2)
Writing a cv to accompany an
  application (2)
Writing a telegram (2)
Doing the crossword (2)
Writing a job application (2)
Making pre-presentation notes (2)
Writing an advertisement (7)
Writing poetry (7)
Filling in forms (7)
Completing official documents (7)
Journalism (6)
Writing a recipe down (5)
Writing an invitation (4)
Prose writing (4)
Report writing (4)
Writing a love letter (3)
Doing an examination (3)
Writing labels (3)
Writing instructions for others (3)
Writing school absence notes (3)
Making notes for an essay (2)
Writing graffiti on a wall (2)

Writing up lecture notes
Writing a seminar paper
Writing speech in cartoons
Taking a phone message
Writing notices
Writing a personal column
Writing for children
Writing a song
Writing a newsletter
Writing down an address
Writing down a proverb
Writing a postcard
Writing out a prescription
Writing a letter to a tutor
Writing a cryptic message
Designing a questionnaire
Entering accounts in a ledger
Subtitling
Making this list
Writing a timetable
Making a summary
Making workcards
Copying a knitting pattern
Writing revision notes
Making a poster
Writing a comprehension
Doing a spelling test
Writing a horoscope
Writing on the blackboard
Writing a complaint
Writing a computer program
Applying for an overdraft

The items in the list are also interesting for two other reasons: they show how brief our writing typically is and how integrated with daily routine. Although there are a number of extended writing types in this list (letters, reports, academic assignments, essays, publishable materials), these are far less common and are usually written for special work- or study-related purposes. Overwhelmingly, the kind of writing we do day in day out is brief, informal and integrated with everyday living rather than separated from it. Classroom writing should surely reflect some of this variety. Before looking further at this question let us turn our attention to the writing process, including its relationship to longer pieces of writing.

The writing process

If we can analyse the different elements that are involved in a longer piece of writing, and can help learners to work through them, become conscious of them, and use this knowledge positively in their own writing, then such writing will have a lot of the stress taken out of it. Tackling one by one the elements which determine what we write down is what process writing is about.

Before reading on, we invite you to perform a simple task connected with process writing. But first, it may help you to think of an analogy in which you compare a piece of writing to a tennis match where the players concentrate on serving, returning from the base-line, net-play, volleying, lobbing, drop-shots and match strategy. Writing, like playing tennis, is an activity made up of several processes, such as thinking what to write and the order to put it in.

Task

Close your book and jot down what you see as the process elements that together make up writing. Do not look at the list below until you have done this.

If you had trouble making up a list, don't worry. You will not be alone! It takes time to get used to analysing the writing process in this way. In any case you may be interested in the following list:

List jotted down by an experienced teacher of writing

- deciding what to say
- thinking about starting
- thinking who we are writing for
- thinking about our aim in writing this particular piece
- thinking about the way it should be set out on the page
- deciding on the order in which we put our ideas
- deciding on paragraphing and sub-headings
- giving it a title
- making sure we have the script right (the right font if word-processing)
- deciding where to put capitals, underlining, italics, quotation marks and other punctuation

- spelling
- choosing words to convey meaning
- finding the best word, most suited to the context
- writing a grammatical sentence
- writing a fluent sentence that reads well
- reading what we have written to see if it reads well
- reading what we have written with another reader in mind
- deleting, adding or changing the text to suit the reader
- proof-reading for small mechanical mistakes, e.g. spelling
- making sufficient interesting points
- illustrating our points to add interest and help understanding
- referring to the ideas of others

Such lists remind us of the many processes that are involved in writing. And if you have difficulty remembering all of them, it's likely that your students will have a much more limited, conscious awareness of process elements. In fact, if you do ask your students about their own writing, they are most likely to speak about deciding what to write and how to get started, while some may go on to talk about details of spelling, grammar, and vocabulary. Those with more experience occasionally mention paragraphing and organisation.

Before moving on to the next section, it may be worthwhile looking at process writing in a wider context. The first thing to be said is that the valuable research done on first language (L1) writing by investigators such as Flower and Hayes in the early 1980s forms a useful basis for researchers into second language (L2) writing. It is generally agreed that there is an important core of similarities between L1 and L2 writing as well as some significant differences. One important line of research into L1 writing explicated in Flower and Hayes (1981) is the cognitive process theory. Researchers into process writing owe much to these ideas. In this book, we assume that there is enough overlap between L1 and L2 writing to make such ideas about process writing useful.

Secondly, it has been assumed that knowing about the processes that go on in a writer's mind provides a useful foundation for teaching. This is, at first, no more than an assumption, but as more and more practitioners (ourselves included) have been able to observe the merits of such an approach and as researchers start to make it their business to measure its effectiveness, so we are able to place more reliance on it. As Silva says:

> The teacher's role is to help students develop viable strategies for
> getting started (finding topics, generating ideas and information,
> focusing, and planning structure and procedure), for drafting

(encouraging multiple drafts), for revising (adding, deleting, mod-
ifying, and rearranging ideas) and for editing (attending to vocabulary, sentence structure, grammar and mechanics). (1990:15)

The most noticeable omission is 'evaluating' which may, of course, be
implied in 'revising'.

Thirdly, we have to take into account the fact that in addition to
the process approaches, there are other ways of teaching writing,
particularly the 'interactive' and the 'social constructionist' approaches.
(Johns 1990:25) The interactive view sees the text as being created by
writer and reader together. The social constructionist view envisages a
discourse community such as a group of those knowledgeable about
chemistry writing for each other. While we find the process approach
the most useful base to work from, our emphasis on the importance of
the reader owes something to the interactive approach. Furthermore,
while social constructionist views have chiefly influenced the teaching
of English for Special Purposes, they are also a reminder that writing
takes place in a community and is not just an individual act.

Finally, a number of writers have stressed the recursive, non-linear
nature of writing, as is made clear in the following quotation:

Planning is not a unitary stage but a distinctive thinking process
which writers use over and over during composition. (Zamel
1983)

Let us sum up these points. Much valuable work has been done in the
last 20 or 30 years on L1 writing. The work on process writing
particularly from the early 1980s has been used by L2 researchers and
is proving useful for developing teaching programmes. Though more
emphasis has recently been laid on the social nature of writing, this is
not so much a threat to process approaches as an enrichment.

There is no agreed list of writing processes among researchers and
even less agreement about exactly what the writing curriculum should
consist of. However, we have extracted a common core for use in
describing the activities in this book. These are the three pre-writing
processes, planning, targeting and organising, and the four in-writing
processes, drafting, evaluating, editing and rewriting.

In preparation for the next section of the Introduction on the
implications for teaching and as a reminder of much that we have
already touched on, this is how Grabe and Kaplan see the process
approach in practice:

The process approach encourages:
– self-discovery and authorial 'voice';
– meaningful writing on topics of importance (or at least of interest) to
the writer;

- the need to plan out writing as a goal-oriented, contextualised activity;
- invention and pre-writing tasks, and multiple drafting with feedback between drafts;
- a variety of feedback options from real audiences, whether from peers, small groups, and/or the teacher, through conferencing, or through other formative evaluation;
- free writing and journal writing as alternative means of generating writing and developing written expression, overcoming writer's block;
- content information and personal expression as more important than final grammar and usage;
- the idea that writing is multiply-recursive rather than linear as a process – tasks are repeated alternatively as often as necessary;
- students' awareness of the writing process and of notions such as audience, voice, plans. (1996:87)

In this section, we have mentioned the work of several researchers. If you want to follow up recent research in the field, you will find William Grabe and Robert Kaplan's book *Theory and Practice of Writing* (from which we have just quoted) extremely useful. We also referred to the work of Tony Silva and Ann Johns, which you will find in a very useful collection of articles *Second Language Writing: Research Insights for the Classroom* edited by Barbara Kroll.

2 Implications for the teaching of writing

Approaches to the teaching of writing

For many years the teaching of writing was neglected as a result of concentration on the aural/oral approach. This was partly the influence of the linguists mentioned on page 1 who treated spoken language as of primary and written language as of secondary importance, and partly the results of theories of learning which set great store by oral repetition. Of course, it is also true that there was a specific demand for courses in spoken rather than written English both for business and from those who found that better and cheaper travel facilities allowed them to study in or go on holiday to English-speaking countries. Their first necessity was to have enough spoken language to survive in that situation. However, while no one would deny the importance of spoken language, this is no reason to neglect the equally important written mode.

One aspect of the theories of learning mentioned above was the development of several methodologies, of which the Direct method and the Audio-lingual method (which relied heavily on much repetitive work in the language laboratory) are good early examples. They both regarded writing as a means of reinforcing what had already been learnt in the speaking phases of lessons. In addition, the exercises in the Audio-lingual method focused on absolute correctness rather than communication. This kind of activity, which we will call 'writing things down', is of course used as an aid to language learning (particularly at the beginner and lower elementary level) and must be clearly distinguished from composing (i.e. writing as a skill enabling us to say what we wish to) for which some language knowledge is required. The widespread adoption of Communicative Language Teaching was one of the major reasons for the recognition of the real importance of teaching writing as a skill. This method, moreover, played a useful role in guiding us to analyse how we do things (i.e. the processes we use) and to recognise the importance of intelligibility and very often also of persuasiveness when communicating through writing.

Teachers who appreciate the importance of Communicative Language Teaching have also found that successful learners need to master a variety of genres or types of writing. Each genre has its own conventions concerned with the type of information to include and the order to put it in. Discussing such conventions helps to provide a clear framework within which students can write effectively.

Let us finish our brief survey on approaches to the teaching of writing with a few words about coursebooks. Coursebooks reflect to a very limited extent changing ideas about successful approaches to teaching writing. They mostly use writing as a supplementary activity to reinforce language learning. Typical examples of coursebook writing activities include gap-filling, writing questions, expanding sentences by adding forms such as adverbs or adjectives, writing about topics such as *classmates* or *the past*, and writing down what is heard on cassette. The best coursebooks try to integrate where possible the skills of writing, reading, listening and speaking, which we are much in agreement with, but they do not always have a clear focus on single skills such as writing. From our experience of coursebooks in several parts of the world, there is often a distinction between international and national coursebooks, the latter providing more writing topics by not trying so hard to integrate all the aspects of the language. This can be useful for a teacher devising a writing course.

Perhaps the most surprising thing about most coursebooks is that even where the official policy is to teach process writing (which is increasingly the case), the coursebooks themselves give very little guidance on how to do this.

Taking writing in the real world into account

When we teach writing, we are not always rehearsing real-world writing, but this section of the Introduction will be concerned only with this kind of writing. Because we are dealing with early-stage learners, we are looking for types of writing which, in the real world, are brief, relatively unchallenging and within the learners' experience. Here are some ways of finding out what your students do in real life in their first or second language:

– by dictating words like *cooking, neighbours, work, family, telephone* and asking your students to write down (either in English or in their mother tongue) one or more kinds of writing they associate with each keyword;
– by asking your students to make a list of all the kinds of writing they themselves do for which they are the prime readership (e.g. making shopping lists, annotating texts, making action plans);
– by asking your class to make a list of all the kinds of writing they think they will need to do to support their language learning in the special situation they now find themselves in. This often encourages creative responses which you can then build on;
– if you teach adult learners who need English in the workplace, by asking them to list all the writing they already have to do in English (if any), followed by writing in English presently done by others which they expect to do one day themselves;
– by asking your learners to think of all the writing types to which they contribute some part, either in the form of information which is then incorporated into some lengthier text by another writer or as a contributor to a multi-authored text. This obviously works well in business, where reports and documents presenting the public face of the organisation frequently include information contributed by many employees. It also works surprisingly well in schools, since the students list mother-tongue writing types to which they contribute some part.

However you work, the list your class makes will give you a first syllabus to work with. This will be based on personal interest and needs in a way that is beyond any general coursebook.

We consider next how you may implement your functional writing syllabus. Turn back to page 6 and find the list of writing types provided by the students. (A reminder that these were English adult teacher trainers, which may help to explain some of the more unusual items on the list!) Photocopy the list and then take a highlighter and go through it highlighting all the writing types that your early stage writers could do in English. Or, if you prefer, simply note the writing types on a separate piece of paper.

How does your list compare with ours?

making a shopping list	making notes in a diary
writing greetings cards	making notes for the family
writing a recipe down	writing an invitation
writing labels	writing instructions for others
writing graffiti on a wall	signing a cheque
writing a telegram	taking a phone message
doing a spelling test	writing down a proverb
writing a postcard	writing down an address

Notice that this list consists almost entirely of items that have a real-life purpose and are not just classroom exercises. This is the type of writing we call 'functional' writing in this Introduction.

Basically, three issues arise in thinking about teaching functional writing. These are, in increasing order of importance, how to make it authentic, how to make it enjoyable, and how to make sure that the students are learning something useful that they can apply outside the classroom.

Authenticity

From our earlier discussion, we know that writing, if it's to be authentic, transcends time and space, is a means of preserving what would otherwise be forgotten, and filters and shapes experience. So a shopping list, to take the first item in the list above:

- will be drawn up in one place and at one time and acted on in another. This happens in real life and we may well be able to replicate this in the classroom;
- will have to be long enough for our students not to be able to remember it without writing it down;
- should be filtered and shaped. Whatever discussion has gone into, for instance, a list of things needed for a party (*Maria likes crisps – she eats practically nothing else*), the written form should contain just what is needed for shopping (*crisps*) without any unnecessary information. The list should be shaped by some principle, such as grouping all the items to be bought at a particular shop or according to the order in which they are to be bought.

Not surprisingly, a little careful thinking about how to make sure that the writing task is authentic already gives us several ideas for the task we are going to give our learners.

Enjoyment

The second stage in the activity design is to think out ways in which making a list could be a really enjoyable activity. One problem is that what is an enjoyable activity for one person may not be so for another, so that the suggestions we make now are necessarily tentative.

If we decide that items of clothing would interest the students most, here are some possible strategies:

1 Students could make a list of imported products and rate them for quality and desirability against locally produced equivalents.
2 Students could make a wish-list containing, say, an item a year they hoped to buy each year for the next ten years.
3 They could try to decide on a typical year's shopping for someone in the public eye, a politician or a pop star perhaps.
4 They could do the same for themselves, or for a friend or family member.

In making these suggestions, we are not making any very special claims for their quality as ideas. Rather we have shown how a) thinking carefully about the reasons for writing can help us to see how the process of functional writing can be managed, and b) for most students we need to go a little bit beyond the most literal and try to think through ideas that are enjoyable because they contain an element of intellectual challenge, personal involvement, even sometimes humour.

Usefulness and application outside the English classroom

The ability to give shape and coherence to a random list is important in the real world. Therefore, further activities in the classroom to reinforce this skill might well be helpful. For instance, drawing up a list of people who are going on a trip which includes eating out provides the opportunity for shaping in ways as diverse as:

– those who have paid and those who have still to pay;
– alphabetical order;
– meat-eaters and vegetarians;
– pick-up points.

An additional or alternative strategy is simply to brainstorm with the class where in the real world lists are to be found and how they are organised. For homework, try getting the students to look through textbooks in English or the mother tongue to observe where and how lists are used, and to confirm or add to the ideas that emerged in class discussion. Their findings can later be discussed in class or used as the basis of further activities.

Teaching process writing

The final product in writing is important. All of us (and this includes our students) would like to produce final products that are imaginative and accurate, personal and public, fluent and correct. Some teachers ask their students to produce a series of products and hope that constant repetition aided by careful marking and assessment will result eventually in acceptable products, not always realising how interesting and effective much process writing can be.

Other teachers, adopting the same general framework, select an aspect of process writing such as readership and ask the students to bear this particularly in mind while writing, and then concentrate on this aspect when grading the work. This is at times a useful strategy and certainly overlaps with process writing proper.

But process writing proper typically makes one aspect of the writing process the central focus of a lesson, and builds an activity round it. It should wherever possible be followed by an opportunity for the students to discuss the writing process. Care must be taken to encourage students to ensure that this new awareness makes a difference on the next occasion when a writing product is required, whether this is in the writing class, elsewhere in the institution, or in the outside world.

Having looked earlier at elements of the writing process, let us consider some of the process decisions facing a student who has been given the task on a particular occasion of producing a substantial piece of writing.

An important element, although not always obvious to students, is determining *purpose* in writing. Outside the classroom, there is usually one main purpose in writing. For instance, we feel strongly on a subject and write a letter with the express purpose of making our views known to someone else. Or we make a shopping list before going to the supermarket so that we don't forget essential items. In the classroom, there may be other purposes, such as the desire to fulfil institutional requirements, to develop language skills, or to produce a piece for continuous assessment. It is worth getting students to ask themselves why they are embarking on each piece of writing that they do.

Having decided on purpose, we need to decide on the *main ideas* we want to write about. Recently an English-speaking learner of Italian was heard to say: 'I'm not sure what on earth to write about even if we had to do it in English.' So we need techniques for deciding on the main ideas. It is obviously useful to know a little about the topic through previous reading, discussion, or experience. However, the best ways of actually gathering ideas and selecting from them are still the simplest. These include:

– brainstorming and then highlighting important points;
– discussing ideas with colleagues;
– taking stock of what we have written at regular intervals as we write and considering what we might go on to write about.

The last point is worth noticing particularly. It reminds us that we sometimes discover what our main ideas are while we are writing our first draft. And sometimes, of course, when writing in a second language, we have to modify our main ideas to suit the language at our disposal; but this, too, is an interesting creative challenge.

Taking note of *readership* is another important part of the writing process. Especially in the early stages of writing, learners may not naturally be conscious of their readership. They appear to be intent on survival – in getting down something reasonably correct in another language. But even at that stage, our students' recognition of readership is shown by their response to our mentioning that the writing may be displayed on the wall and be seen by their classmates, or be read by another teacher, or that pen-friends may be found for learners who have written letters introducing themselves. Learners often say under such circumstances that they would have written differently if they had known who would be reading their work. And it is not only that they would have tried harder to make their work presentable, they would frequently have liked to change the content or the way they arranged it. It is therefore important for students and teachers to make a point of discussing readership whenever possible.

Having looked at three aspects of the writing process which make it easier to put pen to paper confidently – determining purpose, selecting main ideas, and identifying readership – let us now look at a fourth aspect. This is the search for a *suitable form*. This becomes much easier if we distinguish what is conventional from what writers are free to choose for themselves. The beginnings and endings of letters, for example, are conventional. So we might provide a variety of different examples from which our learners could select the most appropriate for their own purpose. This kind of activity gives the learner the confidence to start writing. Another way to give learners the confidence to start is to remind them that they can consider what would best suit the topic and the reader part-way through, or even sometimes at the end of, their first draft.

Disregarding for the moment how we start and finish, at this level most pieces of writing will have their contents organised chronologically (as in storytelling), or from general to particular (as in describing a place), or from most important to least important (as in making a complaint), or working up to some logical conclusion (as in an argument or scientific investigation). Although we can make simple generalisations such as these about what happens most regularly in a particular kind of writing, each piece of writing will nevertheless develop its own organisation, which may from time to time depart with good reason from these expected norms. One task in the classroom will be to make students aware of the types of arrangement open to them. We will have succeeded best not by making students copy someone else's arrangement, but by determining what best suits their purpose.

Furthermore, as we write, we may feel that we need to develop a particular argument or illustrate a point or make something clearer. Revision and addition may be part of drafting so that we delete and insert as we draft. While this is easier with a computer, revision is not difficult by hand if the draft is written on alternate lines.

It is even possible to postpone the beginning of a piece of writing till we are sufficiently into it to know whether we want a beginning that catches the reader's attention, that sets out what the rest of the piece of writing is about, or that relates very specifically to readers and their interests. One way of putting this into practice in the classroom is to provide examples of other students' writing without their first paragraphs, asking the students to supply a suitable first paragraph themselves. Or students who are struggling to start can be encouraged to get on with the body of the work and then to add or refine the first paragraph as their last task.

When we re-read our own work, we start to discover ambiguities, wordiness, lack of connectives, lack of clarity, and, of course, errors. Furthermore, if we imagine ourselves to be other potential readers, we will realise we have sometimes provided too much detail for such readers or too little. It is often a help to sleep on a draft before coming back to it. Reading in this way is sometimes referred to as *evaluation* and writing a second draft is referred to as *rewriting*. It is, of course, also possible for the teacher or for other learners to assist in such evaluation. Often it is useful to proof-read for minor errors separately from the re-reading referred to above – this is a particularly useful pair-activity in class.

To sum up, there are two central things to bear in mind in teaching process writing. The first is that writers reach their final product by working hard at giving expression to what they want to say by the best possible means at their disposal. It is an organic process which does not depend on copying a model. While extensive reading over a period of time provides a background for the writer, copying the ideas, wording, or formats of texts is no substitute for the process of struggling to find the best expression for what the writer wants to say. The writer's own product is paramount. Though it may sometimes be easier for us to present a model product to be imitated, it is more effective in the end to help learners to express what they really want to say in their own best possible way. Even at the stage of rewriting, we need to be careful not to impose a 'correct' version which does not fully express the learner's intentions. Our role is to be a facilitator and fellow writer rather than a knowledgeable expert at one remove from our learners.

The second point is that, having analysed the elements involved in the writing process as we have done above, we need to create activities that teach these elements. Such activities must be interesting, draw on the existing knowledge, interests, and abilities of learners, and result in greater awareness of the writing process and greater writing skill. A writer who has participated in an activity on taking readership into consideration (such as Section 4.3 where the students draw their target reader), and who has reflected on it, is unlikely not to take readership into account when writing on future occasions.

We do not claim to have provided an exhaustive list of the elements that make up the writing process. In fact, these elements do not follow one another neatly in stages, but are interconnected and at times operate in parallel rather than serially. However, we ourselves have found that focusing on one element at a time has really helped our students. In doing so, we are not so much teaching students to write as raising their awareness of what it takes to be a good writer. This enables them to know what they are doing when they write and thus gives them confidence. Section 5, which is our suggestion for a self-contained process-writing course, has awareness raising written into it – in fact, it is an exercise in writing about writing.

Because attention to the process of writing is so important, we have also indicated for each activity the process stage/s most likely to be practised in it. For simplicity's sake, we have reduced these to seven: *planning, targeting, organising, drafting, evaluating, editing,* and *rewriting.*

Perhaps you would like to leaf through two or three activities at this point to get an indication of how you can teach the writing process to your own students.

Finally, it is worth noting that process writing leads naturally to self-assessment, discussion with classmates, and even to peer-assessment. Process writing implies that evaluation and feedback will be useful because they occur within the writing process and are frequently carried out by the writers themselves. This way, writers can improve their writing before it goes out into the world to stand or fall on its merits. Further discussion of this issue and the activities connected with it are to be found in Section 8.

3 A guide to the writing activities in this book

This book contains approximately a hundred activities which together form a complete writing programme. In this section we try to answer the questions that you may want to ask about the activities.

Do I need to work my way through all the activities in this book?
By no means. Choose your own selection of activities. It is a good idea to make a rough choice and then be prepared to change some of your original choices as your course progresses. You will best know what suits the needs of the students and what you will be comfortable teaching. Be prepared to take some risks, and to add activities of your own.

Do I need a lot of special equipment?
Basically, no. It is very helpful to have access to a photocopier and some means of fixing your students' written work onto the wall. Some activities are slightly easier if you have an overhead projector as well as a blackboard or whiteboard. You and your students will need plenty of loose-leaf paper, but very often small pieces of paper or scrap paper used on one side will do. For only a small number of the exercises in Section 6 are computers essential.

What kind of class organisation is required?
There is a lot of pairwork and groupwork, to allow the students to discuss each other's ideas, look constructively at each other's work, and even collaborate on the writing tasks. This does not imply that students are never expected to work on their own. However, the more flexible the classroom the better, and at the very least students should be able, when required to, to work in pairs.

What do I do while my students are engaged in groupwork?
Don't be afraid to join in as a group member as long as you are able to join in on the same terms as everyone else. Observe what is going on, but don't hover on the edge of groups or you'll change the way your students work. Be sure to give genuine opinions and responses. Your observation of what is going on in the groups may be useful in planning subsequent lessons.

Will there always be a piece of written work I have to mark?
By no means. Because the activities are learning experiences, some will simply raise your students' consciousness of one element of writing, such as ways of selecting the best material to write about. Students will do a lot of self-evaluation and evaluation in pairs. There are, however, activities, especially in Section 7, some of which result in extended pieces of writing, which are among those which your institution or yourself will probably want to grade.

What information is given about each activity?
You may wish to glance at one or two activities either before or after you read this section.

Level: a 1–10 scale (where 1 = suitable for beginners and 10 = suitable for higher intermediate students) of how difficult the activity is. The arrow indicates that it is suitable for the suggested level and for levels of students above this level

Time: the approximate length of time it takes to complete the activity

Materials: any materials other than a blackboard and pencil and paper

Process stage: the process stage/s which the activity focuses on. One or more of *planning, targeting, organising, drafting, evaluating, editing, rewriting*

Rationale: what the activity should achieve and why

Procedure: the way the activity is to be carried out in the classroom

Follow-up: subsequent optional writing exercises that lead naturally out of the activity

Variation/s: where there are interesting and useful other ways of teaching the same activity we note them in order of difficulty

Comment/s: further miscellaneous notes that gloss the activity

Where do I find the input for these activities?
As often as not you will be able to draw on the existing knowledge and experience of the students themselves.

Are there any suggestions for teaching Roman script to learners who are unfamiliar with it?
A number of ideas about teaching script are added to the end of each activity in Section 2.

Is there an easy way of finding the right activity for my class?
Use the Contents page, which indicates the level, and the Indexes, which list activities by function.

1 From copying to writing

Most early-stage writing is a form of copying, and is as much about using writing to support language learning as about teaching writing itself. The copying-with-a-difference activities in this section are intended to be more creative than those you may have come across before. Some also involve an element of dictation so that the students copy or write down what their teacher has composed orally. The activities are arranged with the simpler ones at the beginning of the chapter and the more challenging ones at the end.

1.1   Overwriting   Level 1↑

Time   15 minutes
Process stage   Editing

Rationale

Overwriting is a technique whereby the students write on top of an existing script. It allows them to practise writing in a totally safe situation.

Procedure

Write two or three sentences on the board and invite students who see any word(s) whose meaning they don't know to come up and overwrite the word(s) concerned. So if three students don't know the word *cable* and one student doesn't know the word *Ocean* in the sentence *On Sunday we were at Ocean Park and went on the cable car* and come up to overwrite them, the sentence on the board will look like this:

On Sunday we were at Ocean Park
and went on the cable car

In this way, you can identify unknown vocabulary and then use your usual method of teaching it.

Variations

i   You can get your students to work in small groups. Distribute photocopies of the text they are to overwrite.

ii The students can overwrite everything they know and then go back to what they don't know and either try to guess the word's meaning or replace it with a word they know that makes sense.

iii Use this technique to practise writing single words on a list of words – each student chooses which word(s) they want to overwrite (and says why).

iv The class can write a story word-by-word – each student overwrites the word written by the last student and then adds their own next word.

v   Combine overwriting with listening comprehension – play a verse of a song and ask a student to come and write the words they heard in the right places on the board. Play the song again and ask another student to overwrite words they agree with and write in any new ones not written up by the previous student, etc.

Comment

This activity is particularly good for focusing on script when you have learners unfamiliar with the Roman alphabet.

1.2   Making word lists   Level 1↑

Time   15 minutes

Materials   Coursebook, class reader or other text

Process stage   Editing

Rationale

Making word lists by copying out of the coursebook is the simplest kind of writing activity, but if you choose the criterion for making the list carefully enough, it can be a challenging learner activity. For example, if you asked the students to make a list of all the words in a coursebook unit for which there are homophones (*by/buy*, *I/eye*, etc.), they would probably find this quite difficult. Or if you asked them to make a list of all the two-letter words, how many would be able to tell you in advance that almost all two letter words (*an*, *to*, *of*, etc.) have more grammatical function than lexical salience?

Procedure

Specify a text (a unit in the coursebook or a chapter in the reader, for example) and ask the students to copy down words in a certain category. The category will depend on the level of your students. Good categories include two-letter words, three-letter words, words ending in inflectional morphemes such as *-ing* and *-ed*, or in derivational morphemes such as *-er*, *-ness*, *-ly* and *-wise*, words with prefixes, words with initial capital letters, nouns that have cognate verbs (*advice/advise*, *work* [n]/*worker*/*work* [vb]), time words, activity words, personal and place names, colloquial expressions, words relating to people, to occupations, to home, to travel, words you don't understand. The list is endless.

Follow-up

You will then be able to use these lists in your regular teaching. You can also add to existing lists from time to time.

Comment

This is the simplest kind of copying activity, but it enables the students to teach themselves quite a lot about English as they do it. If you teach intermediate-level students, from time to time you can ask them to write about what they have learnt from their word lists.

1.3 Planning ahead   Level 1↑

Time 30–40 minutes

Materials Next week's television schedule

Process stage Editing

This activity is appropriate if you are living in a country where there are English-language television programmes. And probably there are newspapers or magazines that list the programmes to be shown during the coming week. In this activity, the students draw up their own English-language viewing schedule.

Rationale

Although we know that our students are in competition with other members of their family for use of the television, this select-and-copy activity encourages them to watch English-language television and helps their family to recognise its importance as a language learning aid. The students have to copy programme titles and then during the next few days they and their families refer to the student's writing which will be left in a prominent place at home. So this is public rather than casual writing.

Preparation

Either ask the students to bring a copy of the week's television schedule to class on Monday or make copies of it for them.

Procedure

1 Each student should study the television schedule and choose at least one English-language programme which they would like to watch each evening during the week. As they make their decisions, they should write them down using a formula such as *On Tuesday I plan to watch ...* .
2 Allow time for the students to compare and discuss their choices in small groups.

Follow-up

Encourage your students to watch the programmes they have selected and allow class time for comments and discussion on them.

Variations

i You can also ask your students to give a reason for each choice.
ii There are other similar possibilities for expanding newspaper information. For example, cinema and sports schedules can be treated in the same way and allow for the possibility of introducing modals like *I would like to ...* .

1.4 Coursebook collages

Level 1↑

Time   40 minutes upwards

Materials   Coursebook; A3 paper

Process stage   Organising

Rationale

Coursebooks are written to be predictable. Collages are collections of items taken from a variety of sources and grouped together in new and striking ways. If you take items out of context (for example, headings such as *Negatives* or *Short answers*), they often assume a more universal significance. And when you put two items together, you often get a surprisingly pleasing effect (for example, *What's your telephone number?*, *With or without lemon?*).

Procedure

Tell your students that they have 40 minutes to make a collage on a sheet of A3 paper using any of the materials in their coursebooks from single words to whole paragraphs. They will have to decide which materials to use and where to place them on the collage, and then to copy them out. They should be reproduced as they appear in the coursebook. The results make nice wall displays and are especially good to read.

Variations

i If you have a roll of lining paper and a small class, you can blu-tack the paper to a wall and each student can make their collage on one part of the paper.

ii A more ambitious variation for intermediate-level students is to try and make a prose poem out of items selected from the coursebook and recombined in original ways.

1.5   Deleting the inapplicable   Level 2↑

Time   30 minutes

Materials   3–4 texts (see *Preparation*)

Process stage   Editing

Rationale

The simplest of all creative copying tasks is to copy a text and at the same time delete any items which do not apply to you. Try this for yourself with the set of texts in one of the boxes at the end of the activity. First scan each text in the box and choose the one closest to your own experience. Then simply delete anything in your chosen text which is not true for you. The result is your own new text, yet it hasn't involved you in writing anything.

Preparation

Prepare three or preferably four texts which describe the same event – having a holiday, spending a weekend at home, going on a shopping trip, celebrating the New Year, going to a party. You will probably need to write these texts yourself, although you can sometimes use the compositions written by students or coursebook texts. Or if it's more convenient, try the texts supplied at the end of this activity. The texts you use need to contain quite a lot which will be true for your students and some things which won't. Make a copy of all the texts for each student.

Procedure

1 Distribute the texts and explain that each student should scan them quickly and decide which comes closest to their own experience.
2 Working with this text, each student should delete all the parts of the text which are not true for themselves. So if the first sentence were *I get up at six o'clock each morning*, they would only need to delete *at six o'clock* (unless of course that was true for them too).
3 Ask the students to copy the resulting text into their exercise books.
4 Allow time for the students to gather in small groups and show each other their texts.

Shopping experiences

A visit to the supermarket

I usually go to the supermarket by car. Sometimes I go alone, sometimes with my family. I like to see what's new in the supermarket. I always have an idea of what to buy before we go, and sometimes I even make a shopping list. I like the shelves which sell biscuits, crisps, soft drinks and chocolate. I don't like the shelves that sell smelly things like meat, fish and cheese. The most boring shelves are those that sell soap powder and cleaning things. I like to choose something I hadn't planned to buy. And I hate waiting in the queue at the checkout. When the queue's very long, I sometimes feel like leaving my trolley and just walking out without my shopping. I feel sorry for the people working on the checkouts. It must be very boring and it's non-stop work. I try to be as friendly to them as possible.

Window shopping

There are some shops that I never go into, but I always look in their windows. Especially I do this with jewellers. I like looking at the beautiful rings, necklaces and watches, but I can never afford to buy any of them. Sometimes I go window shopping for clothes – again, I just look at the displays in the windows of the boutiques, but I'm hardly ever brave enough to go into the shops. I prefer department stores because you can look at things and even touch them without having to buy anything. I like nice clothes and shoes and often think how good I'd look if I wore them. Sometimes I see something I really like – and when I go back later and it's gone, I feel sad. I like window shopping most in other countries because it's interesting. I know I haven't much money to spend and I'm often looking for presents for my friends and family.

Going shopping together

I like going shopping with my friends, but I hate going shopping with my family. When I go with my friends, I like to see them buying things. If they are happy, it makes me happy too. We tell each other how good we would look in all the clothes we see. Sometimes we go for a meal or drink together when we're out shopping – this is always a happy time. But when I go shopping with my family, it's different. Sometimes I go with my mother, sometimes I go with my father, sometimes I go with my brother, sometimes I go with my sister. But it doesn't matter who I go with, they never want to look at what I want to look at. And, worse still, they always want me to look at what they want to look at. It's boring. Worst of all is when they want to buy me something I really don't like.

Trying clothes on

I like trying clothes on, especially in shops where you can just take two or three things and try them on without a shop assistant 'helping' you. But I don't like trying things on in shops where an assistant waits for you outside the changing room. I know they want me to feel guilty enough to buy what I'm trying on. When I try things on, I always try to wear something that I've bought recently and need to match. I never leave anything valuable in the changing room, even for a minute. I'm always careful about the light – often the bright lights in the changing room make the clothes look much better than they really are. I try never to buy anything that doesn't feel comfortable and make me look good. And I always check to make sure that what I've tried on is properly made before I go to pay for it. But most of the things I try on, I don't buy.

The market

There are some things I would never buy in the market, other things that I always buy in the market and some things that I sometimes buy in the market and sometimes buy in the supermarket. I never buy meat in the market because it always smells, but I always buy fish there because it's fresh. I often buy fruit in the market, but I usually look at or even ask about the prices at a number of stalls before buying. I often go to the same market stall for fruit because they know me there and don't give me all the stuff they want to get rid of. I like the market best when there aren't too many people there because then it's easier to buy. But some people only go to the market when it's busy because they like the atmosphere then. I think I'm quite good at bargaining.

© Cambridge University Press 1998

Variations

i   Themes other than events also make good topics, e.g. *My family, My appearance, My home*.
ii As well as redundant word deletion, other deletion activities include deleting sentences that are boring or too long. Often what is deleted can be used as the raw material of another piece of writing.
iii It's also possible to expand the text resulting from this activity by adding more detail to the abbreviated description or substituting viable words for those that have been deleted.

Comment

Deleting is usually the prerogative of the teacher, so it's nice to extend it to the students for a change!

Getting up in the morning

Arthur's routine I stumble out of bed at 6.45 a.m., put on my dressing-gown, but not my slippers, go to the toilet, and go downstairs to make a cup of tea. After I switch the kettle on, I collect the milk from the front door and the newspaper if it has arrived. I take a cup of tea to my wife in bed and then shave with an electric razor while drinking my own tea and starting to do today's crossword puzzle. Finally I have a shower and get dressed.

Eleanor's routine When the alarm clock wakes me up, I put the radio on and lie in bed for a while looking at the ceiling. I prefer to get dressed before going to the bathroom. After washing, I go downstairs and start to get things together for my packed lunch – drink, fruit, biscuit, crisps. I buy a sandwich at school. I have a small breakfast, then go upstairs to brush my teeth and finish packing my school-bag. Then I say goodbye to my mum. Sometimes I walk to school and sometimes my dad gives me a lift.

Janet's routine I usually wake up before my alarm clock goes off. I stretch in bed and think about the day ahead. I get out of bed at the same time each day and look out of the window. I put breakfast TV on while I'm getting dressed. Most mornings I put my shorts and running shoes on and go for a ten-minute jog. Then I have a shower and put my working clothes on. Breakfast is a cup of coffee or tea, and bread or toast. I do my make-up and then drive to work. I always check that I look good in the car mirror, and then leave the car in the car park and walk up to the office.

Peter's routine I finish my breakfast, do the washing up, pack my bag, clean my teeth again, and then I think about getting to work. It takes me forty minutes to get to work. The lift's never at my floor because my neighbour leaves an hour before me. There are always people waiting for the minibus. I buy a paper at the station and then read it on the train. As there's a train every three minutes, I never have to wait long. The train journey takes about twenty minutes. From the station it's a three-minute walk to my office – I walk out of the station, down a level, and then over the footbridge which crosses the main road and directly onto the campus. Another day!

© Cambridge University Press 1998

1.6 Where and when – writing questions   Level 2↑

Time   30 minutes

Process stage   Editing

Preparation

You will need to think of a number of thought-provoking questions which are suitable for your students' language level and experience. They should be questions which could be introduced by either *Where* or *When*. Possible questions include:

– Where/When did you see your brightest moon?
– Where/When did you have your closest brush with death?
– Where/When did you first fall in love?
– Where/When did you last lose your temper?
– Where/When did you last cry?
– Where/When did you last go swimming?
– Where/When did you eat the best meal of your life?
– Where/When did you last buy yourself a present?
– Where/When did you last tell a joke?
– Where/When did you first take a photograph?
– Where/When did you first meet your best friend?
– Where/When were you really happy?
– Where/When did you last complain about something?
– Where/When did you last send a postcard?
– Where/When did you first use a computer?
– Where/When did you last buy something extravagant?

Procedure

1 Dictate the questions you have thought of to your students.
2 Pair the students and ask them to take turns deciding which question they would like their partner to ask them. They should specify whether they would prefer the *when* or *where* version and explain why.

1.7 Copying a story

Level 3↑

Time 45 minutes

Materials Photocopies of a short story or piece of informative writing

Process stages Drafting; writing from memory

Rationale

Most copying from printed material in the real world is a two-stage process: first we must read and understand the original text, and then that understood meaning is encoded as our own written text. It is at this second stage that grammar and spelling errors sometimes occur. Copying plays an important role in developing accurate writing skills.

Preparation

Choose a text which can be divided into four equal sections, each three or four sentences long. Short stories work well. Make sufficient copies for each student to receive one section.

Procedure

1 Divide the class into groups of four. Hand out a different part of the prepared text face downward to each member of the group.
2 Explain that each student will be copying down what is on the other side of the paper and that no writing is permitted while the print is visible. The paper can be turned over as often and for as long as is required, but each time writing takes place, the blank side of the paper must be uppermost.
3 The students then share their own copied section with the other group members who work out the correct order of the four sections of text. Once the correct order has been determined, the sections should be pasted together and given a title.

Variations

i Another option is to have the students read aloud what they are writing so that the other members of their group write it down too.
ii With a small class, you may prefer to put the sections of writing on the wall so that each learner has to go over, look, remember, and then sit and write.
iii You can also get the students to read sentences that are upside down, or seen in the mirror, or flashed (shown only for a very brief time so that only part of them can be deciphered reliably or remembered fully).

1.8   Rewriting class readers – modifying text

Level 3↑

> **Time**   Best as an out-of-class activity
>
> **Materials**   Class reader or individual reader
>
> **Process stage**   Rewriting

Procedure

Work with a short, simplified reader. Each time the reader is read, ask the students to copy out part of it for homework, making whatever changes they think are needed to make the text a truer reflection of their own culture or experience. You will need to specify how much they should copy or whether they should copy some particular part. Thus a student from Hong Kong would rewrite a sentence like *The journey from the city centre to the airport lasted for an hour and took us through miles of open country* as *The journey from Central to the airport took us under the harbour and over the new suspension bridges. It was very quick – 20 minutes.*

1.9   Personalising the coursebook   Level 3↑

Time   10–15 minutes

Materials   Coursebook dialogues and descriptions of people

Process stage   Rewriting

Rationale

This activity is one way of making the textbook relevant to the students as people as well as language learners. At the same time an important aspect of the writing process is practised.

Procedure

1 If you are working with a dialogue, ask the students to imagine the dialogue takes place between themselves and either a friend or colleague at work or a family member. They should rewrite the dialogue to make it as authentic as possible.
2 The results of this activity make nice wall displays.

Variations

i A good variation is to ask the students to copy the dialogue out as neatly as possible (alternatively, enlarge and photocopy the dialogue if this is permitted) and then write in sentences which attempt to explain a) why the characters say what they say, and b) what they mean by what they say. The students can also write in what they would have said under the circumstances, together with their reasons. There is an example on the next page.
ii If you are working with a description of a person rather than a dialogue, the students should imagine the person is themselves or someone they know well and rewrite the description to make it as accurate a portrait as possible.

B *doesn't want*
A *to go*

→ **A:** I'm going to hitchhike round the world.

B: Oh, that's very dangerous.

A: No, it isn't. I'll be all right.

↘ **B:** Where will you sleep?

I'll find somewhere. (this sounds better)

A: ~~Oh, I don't know.~~ In youth hostels. Cheap hotels.

↗ **B:** You'll get lost.

B *doesn't want*
A *to go*

A: No, I won't. *I never get lost. (not so strong)*

↘ **B:** You won't get lifts.

A: Yes, I will. *I'm usually lucky. (not so strong)*

↘ **B:** What will you do for money?

A: I'll take money with me.

↘ **B:** You haven't got enough.

A: If I need money, I'll find jobs.

↗ **B:** Well ... are you sure you'll be all right?

B *realises she can't persuade A not to go*

A: Of course I'll be all right.

↖ *A thinks B is being silly – she worries too much*

....

1.10   Creative copying

Level 3↑

Time   30 minutes

Process stages   Drafting; rewriting

....

Rationale

The purpose of this activity is to show students that it's relatively easy to write striking sentences in English.

Preparation

You will need to think up 5–6 model sentences to dictate. There are some examples on the next page.

– I want to <u>write</u> like <u>Shakespeare</u>.
– Who wants to <u>eat</u> like the <u>English</u>?
– <u>Writing</u> in <u>English</u> is difficult.
– I prefer <u>Sunday morning</u> to <u>Saturday night</u>.
– <u>A bird in the hand</u> is worth two <u>in the bush</u>.
– There's no <u>time</u> like <u>the present</u>.
– When a man is tired of London, he is tired of life.
– You can lead a <u>horse</u> to <u>water</u> but you can't make it <u>drink</u>.
– There's no place like <u>home</u>.
– <u>Variety</u> is the <u>spice</u> of life.
– Whatever <u>will be, will be</u>.
– <u>Tomorrow</u> never comes.

Procedure

1 Explain that you are going to dictate a number of short sentences. The students are to write down their own adapted versions. They should retain the original structure but replace one or more words or phrases in each sentence. Provide an example such as *A change is as good as a rest*. Ask the students to make suggestions for a version in which *change* and *rest* are replaced. Explain that as you dictate, the students may write down your sentence and then their own adaptation, or may write their own adaptation straight away.
2 Dictate each sentence, allowing sufficient time for most of the students to write down an adaptation.
3 After you have dictated all your sentences, allow two or three minutes for checking and for the students to write down adaptations for any sentences that they didn't complete during the dictation phase.
4 Ask the students to work in small groups and select especially effective sentences to read to the rest of the class.
5 You can often make a really good wall display with the most striking sentences. Display them in prominent positions around the classroom.

Variations

i You can dictate and then write the sentences on the board, indicating which items should be replaced. The underlined words in the list of sentences in *Preparation* are suggestions for replaceable items.
ii Another variation is to pair students. When you dictate a sentence, indicate which words/phrases should be replaced. One student

brainstorms as many words as possible to replace the first word and the other student brainstorms as many words as possible to replace the second word. So in *A change is as good as a rest*, one student would be brainstorming words to replace *change*, the other words to replace *rest*. Then ask the students to work together and see how many good sentences they can make with the words they have brainstormed.

iii You can also use lines from poetry which can be adapted to suit the classroom itself, such as Ted Hughes's *Through the window I see no star* (the students replace *star*). Or make up your own lines, such as *And on the wall I dreamt there was a piece of apple pie* (the students replace *piece of apple pie*).

1.11   Expanding outlines

Level 3⬆

Time   30 minutes

Materials   A story outline (see *Preparation*)

Process stage   Drafting

Rationale

In this activity, the teacher supplies a minimal outline and the students enrich it.

Preparation

You will need to invent a simple three-sentence story which your students can expand in a virtually infinite number of ways while still keeping to three sentences. There are some examples on the next page.

Procedure

1 Discuss the fact that sometimes we want to write simply, for example *The captain scored*, and sometimes with greater detail, for example *The captain of Newcastle United scored at the beginning of the second half*.
2 Ask the students to work individually or in pairs. Write your outline story on the board and ask each pair to expand each sentence so as to make their own original story.
3 Ask some of the students to read their stories aloud.

The child put his jacket on the chair. A classmate was watching. She took the money.

The plane took off. The writer opened her briefcase. The story was to make her a millionaire.

The glass was empty. The girl watched him. The passenger stood up slowly.

The girls were standing in a group. The sun shone. They were staring at something.

My friend opened the door. The old man was eating. She told him the news.

The boy was wearing jeans. He was talking. The girl looked at the ring.

The woman came out of the building. The car stopped. There were a lot of people.

Follow-up

You can ask one pair to write an outline story for another pair to expand. This is a more difficult exercise than it looks because the students have to write a three-sentence story which is complete but also encourages expansion.

Variations

i   At Step 3, ask the students to arrange themselves in order from the story with the fewest words to the story with the most words, so that the shortest story is read first and the longest story is read last.

ii   Alternatively at Step 3, ask the students to arrange themselves in order from the story with the most words to the story with the fewest words. This way, the activity picks up pace as increasingly shorter stories are read.

iii   You can also ask the students to replace phrases in the outline stories with phrases of their own choice.

iv   The students can also be asked to add sentences, especially in an area you've just been working on. So if you've been teaching time, for example, ask the students to add a sentence involving a time expression; or if you've been teaching relative clauses, ask them to add a relative clause.

1.12 Ordering from a catalogue Level 3↑

Time   60 minutes

Materials   Photocopies of list of presents (see the examples at the end of the activity); for *Variation*, one mail-order shopping catalogue or set of pictures of shopping for every two students

Process stage   Drafting

Rationale

Copying text accurately from an original source is an essential part of both serious and casual writing. This activity provides an authentic reason for copying accurately.

Preparation

Make enough photocopies of the list of presents given at the end of this activity so that there is one for each pair of students.

Procedure

1 Divide the class into groups of four. Ask the groups to imagine that a kind friend or relation wants to give each member of the group a different, rather special birthday present. But there are rules – the presents must be a complete surprise and the following procedures must be followed for choosing them.

2 Each member of the group will be interviewed for five minutes by the other three members of the group, who will ask about the person's interests and lifestyle. The students should take notes as they interview.

3 When the interviews are over, each group must divide into two pairs of students. The pairs should sit on opposite sides of the classroom.

4 Distribute one copy of the list of presents taken from a mail-order catalogue to each pair. The pairs should discuss what they think their fellow students in the group would most enjoy being given.

5 The name and address of the recipient of the gift together with full details of the gift must be supplied. These details include:
   - Name of the item
   - Size, colour, etc.

– Item number
– Price, including any postage and packing
6 Using these guidelines, all students should copy out their choices neatly.
7 Regroup the pairs and allow time for them to discuss the appropriacy of the presents chosen.

Variation

It's worth collecting catalogues from shops and mail-order companies, as well as saving any you come across yourself, so that you can use authentic materials for this activity. If you do this, don't forget to stipulate an upper price limit.

ITEM NO. 123: The Famous Hill-Huggers, as used in the Himalayas – men's and women's walking boots. Available in grey, blue and green. Sizes 34–38, £25.00; 40–46, £28. Add £2.50 post and packing.

ITEM NO. 124: The Execu-case. Look smart with this 100% leatherette briefcase. Choose between burgundy and black. £42.99, or only £45.99 complete with umbrella. Post and packing free UK mainland; please add £5 for overseas orders.

ITEM NO. 125: A one-year subscription to *The English Language Learner* – a new monthly magazine especially for students of English. Separate editions for elementary and advanced levels. £20 UK, £22 overseas (surface mail), £25 airmail.

ITEM NO. 126: A complete set of English newspapers for the day you were born. Find out what was going on in the world on the big day! Choose between a set of individual copies (£20) or a hard-cover book containing the whole set (£25). Post free before 1 May, otherwise add £2. Remember to tell us your birthday!

ITEM NO. 127: The fabulous 'look younger' kit, as advertised on TV. Contains a full range of creams and toiletries chosen by Dr Daisy Spring to keep you looking and feeling young. Please tell us your age and sex. Comes in a special compact. An ideal present. 1 set £30, 2 sets £50, post free.

ITEM NO. 128: Genuine cashmere mixture MacTough sweater. Look smart in one of the sweaters they wear in Scotland. Men's and women's fittings. Choose between thistle pattern (grey-green) and the traditional royal tartan. Small £24.99; medium £26.99; large £28.99.

ITEM NO. 129: Absolutely the best nightwear! One pair of silk pyjamas, one silk nightshirt/nightdress with your initial on the pocket. £29.99 for both. Write stating size, sex and initial.

ITEM NO. 130: For car drivers – the ultimate car sticker. Easy to fix – just clean your car and apply. Choose between 'I'm good at English' and 'Everyone thinks I'm sexy'. £8.99 each, £15 for both.

ITEM NO. 131: The ultimate throw-away picture. Simply peel off the picture when you get bored with it and reveal the one underneath. 10 peel-away pictures of Life in Britain in a beautiful gold frame. Only £44.99. Add £2.99 for post and packing.

ITEM NO. 132: Everything for the tourist intending to visit Britain in a single handsome wallet. Maps, currency guides, theatre programme lists, pictures of the royal family, 7-day London public transport pass, £5 Harrods voucher, a handsome 'Windsor' pen, disposable camera, 'I'm enjoying myself' badge. £49.99 or US$100 – we can post the wallet to you or you can pre-order and pick it up at Heathrow or Gatwick (please specify which).

1.13 Writing portraits
Level 4↑

Time   30–35 minutes in class, plus writing time

Process stages   Planning; organising; drafting

Rationale

In this activity, the students devise a questionnaire, obtain oral answers to their questions, and then write a portrait of the person interviewed based on their questionnaire responses. The activity thus shows how copying/writing may be interwoven with other skills.

Procedure

1 Agree a questionnaire topic with the students. Good topics include *The next ten years in your life, Memories of Christmas, How you spend your time and how you would like to spend it, Lessons learnt from experience, Being alone, Your second-best friend, Animals in your life, A room of your own.* Once you have chosen a topic, agree 5–6 questions with the class and write them up on the board. Each student should copy them down, leaving enough space between each to record answers.

2 Pair the students and ask them to take turns interviewing each other. Encourage them to use the 5–6 questions as a general framework and ask follow-up questions wherever appropriate. Each interviewer should note down the answers given.

3 After the interviews have been conducted, ask each student to write a portrait of their partner based on the information gathered in the interview. The portraits should contain quotations. If you wish, you can specify that this should take the form of direct speech (to give punctuation practice) or reported speech, or both. This phase makes a good homework activity.

Variations

i This activity also works well in small groups. In a group of four, for example, each student is interviewed by the other students. After the four interviews, each student writes a feature on the various perspectives their three colleagues have revealed about the interview topic.

ii This activity can also be done as an out-of-class activity in which native speakers are interviewed. This works best when students interview in pairs.

1.14   Transformation and back-translation   Level 4↑

Time   30 minutes

Materials   Coursebook dialogues

Process stage   Rewriting

Preparation

Choose two simple dialogues from the coursebook. Although simple, they should contain utterances such as *frankly*, *OK*, *sorry*, *good morning*, *sir*, *yes*, *no*, *next please*, *so* that are not readily represented in indirect speech. If you choose dialogues that the students have not yet studied, this makes for a more interesting activity.

Procedure

1 Divide the class into two halves. Give one half one dialogue and the other half the other dialogue to transform into reported speech. The students may work individually or in pairs.
2 Ask each student/pair to exchange their transformed text with a student/pair who had been working on the other text. Each should now try to reconstruct the original dialogue.
3 When the dialogues have been reconstructed, ask the students to discuss the problems they faced with their partners. Raise the more important or interesting cases in whole-class discussion.

Variations

i There are many different ways of transforming dialogues and texts, including adding and substituting words, phrases, clauses, sentences, and transforming the time, the setting, the degree of assertiveness, the perspective. Sometimes, as with this activity, there is the possibility of back-translation, i.e. trying to transform the reported speech back into the original dialogue.
ii For the thinking student, a low-level activity with a good pay-off is copying coursebook dialogues and making whatever small

alterations they feel have large effects. This can be done in pairs and then two pairs can come together to share what they've done.

iii For a more surreal effect, allow the students to insert a word of their choice wherever it sounds interesting, even if it results in an ungrammaticality. *Wh-* words such as *who* and *what* and frequency adverbs such as *always* and *never* work particularly well.

iv If you have really creative students, have them try transforming the non-text parts of their coursebook into dialogue or text. Features such as pictures, diagrams, figures, cartoons, maps, photographs and charts are all real challenges which also allow for interesting back-translations! There are also features such as invitations, forms and lists which your students can transform to fuller texts. Beginner and elementary coursebooks tend to be richer in non-text, so they are a good source.

v Another idea is to write up coursebook activities. Your students can write up the minutes of a roleplay (a suggestion made by Ann Raimes at a teachers' workshop in Hong Kong), or keep a diary if a coursebook character goes on a trip, or write the record of an interview, or write a thank-you note if someone is invited for a meal, etc. In other words, it's often a good idea to think creatively about the kinds of real-world writing that might accompany the situations depicted in coursebooks.

1.15   Copying and correcting   Level 5↑

> **Time**   From 10–30 minutes depending on the text
>
> **Materials**   One or more texts containing non-standard English
>
> **Process stage**   Rewriting

Preparation

You need to find a text which contains a number of examples of obviously bizarre English and make enough copies for each student in your class (or for each pair of students if they work in pairs). Suitable texts are easy to find in countries where English is not the national language, but by no means impossible to find in countries where it is the national language. Instructions supplied with goods manufactured in non-English-speaking countries are a particularly good source of material. Some examples are given at the end of the activity.

Procedure

1 The students can work individually or in pairs. Distribute a prepared text to each student/pair and ask them to produce a corrected copy.
2 Allow time for a short discussion of any language points or problems encountered in the activity. If you are working with a longer text, a wall display is a good idea as it gives the students a chance to see how their classmates have solved the problems.

Variation

Encourage the students to make the corrected copy as authentic looking as possible, so that a label on a tie should look like a label on a tie, a card supplied with a T-shirt should look like a card supplied with a T-shirt, etc. This means that the students will have to pay attention to typeface and font size if they are word-processing or exercise good design skills if they are writing in longhand. Encourage the use of dictionaries.

Comments

It may be that your students will one day be responsible for communicating through English to a critical audience. It's no bad thing for them to see, even at this early stage in their own learning, that mistakes can destroy the credibility of the product or of the person providing the service.

C15 CO LTD

STRONG JEANS GUARANTEED ORIGINAL DENIM
FOR YOUR GREAT SATISFACTION ARE CUT BY
MOST MODERN TECHNIC AND FIT YOUR BODY TO
AT! HIGH CONCEPTUAL MADE OF THE BEST INTO
BLACK ALMOST AT NEW SPICE TRENDED

For many years the Voss shirt. by Paul Voss. has consistently repre – sented a superblevel oftaste. It is and has been a stronghold of quality and style for men and women who believe in clothes that endure season after season.

Inspired by the faded. comfortable character that Voss shirts acquire after years of wear this shirt has been spe – citally tieated to give it a weathered appearance. This special process. exclusive to Voss. does not impair the longevity of the shirt. rather it enhances the supple hand and contour fit that the Voss shirt is known for. This process also guarantees that the shirt retain its shape and size every time it is washed. The subtle variations and nuances of shading that occur in this whirt are what give this shirt its unique personality and are not to be considered as imperfections.

An extraordinary amount of care has gone into the making of this shirt. sith special attention given to every detail – details which include a clean finish on both sides of the shirt so that the inside looks like the outside. As with all pure cottons. this shirt will continue to soften and fade as it becomes better and more personal with age.

FAX

URGENT

TO : MR PETER GRUNDY   FROM : LIM

SORRY EVERYTHING THIS MORNING. AGNES SEND THE WRONG FAX
NUMBER TO HER CLIENT DR WATERS & RECEPTION TOLD ME YOU
ARE MR BEST WHO IS ONE OF MY CLIENT & HE BOOK THE SAME
THING JUST DIFFERENT DATE. YOUR VOICE SEEMS LIKE HIM. SO
OUR COMMUNICATE TOTALLY DIFFERENCE. TERRIBLY SORRY. I ONLY
GIVE YOU 3 FAX INCLUDE THIS ONE YESTERDAY FEB TRIP & THIS
MORNING MAR TRIP

..AFTER CLARIFY BA. YOU CAN RETURN ON MAR FROM LONDON

1.16 Composing texts Level 7↑

Time 60 minutes

Process stages Drafting; evaluating

At the 1996 IATEFL Conference at Keele University, Peta Gray and Mario Rinvolucri ran a writing workshop in which we each wrote about something that had happened to us. We then passed our writing to our neighbour, who wrote down 20 questions that they wanted to ask us about the incident we had described. We all found it surprisingly easy to think of 20 questions to ask. We acknowledge Peta and Mario's idea, which we follow up in a slightly different way here.

Procedure

1 Ask the students to work in groups of three. Each student should write a description of an incident or situation they experienced on one side of a sheet of A4 paper.

2 When the students have finished writing, ask them to pass their writing to the member of the group sitting on their left. Each student then takes a separate sheet of paper and writes 20 questions which they would like to ask the author of the description.

3 When each student has written the 20 questions, they pass the writing back to the original author sitting on their right and the questions on to the student sitting on their left. When each student receives the 20 questions, they write a description of the incident which they hope will match as exactly as possible the one written by the original author.

4 When the descriptions are written, they are passed one more place round the circle to the original author, who then reads them. Allow 15 minutes for group discussion of the activity and the resulting writing. The outcomes often make a good wall display.

Variation

This activity bears some resemblance to Chinese whispers, so that it would be possible to use the second piece of writing as the stimulus for another set of 20 questions which would then lead to a further piece of writing.

2   The mechanics of writing

The activities in this section deal with areas such as spelling, punctuation and layout. The chapter begins with two investigative exercises which do not require any writing at all. The remaining activities progress from guided to solo writing. We have included a *Focus on script* section at the end of each activity for teachers of students whose first language does not use Roman script.

2.1   In search of capitals   Level 4↑

Time   45 minutes

Materials   Pages of English newspapers or pages from the coursebook

Process stage   Evaluation

Rationale

This activity investigates the capitalisation conventions of English, which are important for clarity and acceptability.

Procedure

1 Divide the class into pairs and ask the students to work on a page of their coursebook. (More advanced students can work with a page from a newspaper since they aren't required to understand every word of the text.) Explain that you are on a voyage of discovery to find out exactly how capitals are used in English. Ask one student to identify all the words and phrases in capitals while their partner writes them down. They should ignore the first person pronoun *I* and sentence-initial words. After five minutes, tell the students to reverse roles.

2 After 10–15 minutes ask the class to share information. Find out what the first word or phrase of the first group is and write it on the board or OHP, leaving room for a heading. Take suggestions for

the category names/titles, e.g. names of people. Ask the next pair for another example from their list, and so on round the class till you have 5–10 examples.

3 Continue asking each pair in turn for an example of a new category, name it, and repeat the above procedure.

4 Ask your students to tell you how the conventions in their language differ.

Variation

In addition to the above activities, you may wish to put up the list of conventions with an example of each on the wall of the classroom and add to it whenever you get a valid example from a member of the class.

Focus on script

Ask the students to list all the capital letters they have found in order from the one that they think is most like the corresponding regular letter, for example C–c, to the one that they think is least like the corresponding regular letter, for example G–g. Discuss the differences between print form capitals and regular letters. If time allows, discuss the differences between handwritten capitals and regular letters. Ask the students to work out what capital letters have in common besides size which differentiates them from regular-sized letters.

2.2   Investigating typographical conventions

Level 3↑

Time   60 minutes

Materials   Authentic texts (see *Preparation*); scissors; paste; blank paper/card

Process stage   Evaluating

Preparation

You are going to need two authentic texts with interesting typographic conventions (i.e. appearance or design) for every four students. Suitable texts include a page of a newspaper or magazine, a handbill, a menu, or any other authentic text that employs several typographic conventions.

Procedure

1 Divide the class into groups of four and give each group a copy of the first authentic text. Write up the following list on the board:
   – Colour of type
   – Colour of background
   – Upper and lower case letters
   – Upright fonts
   – Italics
   – Different fonts
   – Font size
   – Emboldening
   – Underlining
   – Spaces and empty lines
   – Lines and boxes
   – Simulation of handwritten script
2 Discuss with the class which of these features can be found in the text. Tip: it helps if you work with the original when you discuss colour of type and background.
3 Distribute scissors, paste, a large sheet of paper and the second text. Each group should cut out examples of the use of different typographical devices and paste them onto the sheet of paper. They should also discuss and note down anything of interest about the typographical devices used – both their form and their purpose.
4 When the work is sufficiently advanced, display the most comprehensive sheet, which will provide examples to refer to.

Variations

i If you have some old coursebooks which can be cut up, they also make good texts.
ii You can also ask the groups to copy the list and write a brief note (in the mother tongue perhaps) about the way each is used in English.

Focus on script

Ask your students to compare two different fonts carefully and to describe a) the differences they notice in the way that particular letters are formed, and b) the ways in which these forms differ from anything that would be found in handwritten script.

2.3   Dictation and commentary – punctuating direct speech

Level 3↑

Time   45 minutes

Process stage   Drafting – representing speech

Rationale

The aim of this activity is to guide students through the punctuation process necessary when representing a conversation in written form.

Procedure

1 Ask two students to come and stand facing each other in front of the board. Draw four speech balloons on the board so as to suggest that the two students are having a four-turn dialogue.

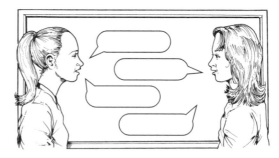

2 Ask the two students to hold a four-turn conversation. Suggest that the first student begins with an invitation or a suggestion. You should write each turn in one of the speech bubbles. So if Karima is talking to Nobuko, you might end up with:

KARIMA: Do you want to come to the cinema with me this evening?

NOBUKO: What's on?

KARIMA: I'm not sure.

NOBUKO: I should do my English homework.

3 You then talk through how you would turn this conversation into a written dialogue. As you talk to yourself, the students should each write down, not your whole think-aloud process, but what you actually decide to write. For example, you might begin: *Do I start KARIMA SAID or KARIMA ASKED NOBUKO – I think I'll start KARIMA ASKED NOBUKO.* (Pause here while the students write down *Karima asked Nobuko.*) *Now I put what Karima actually said in quotation marks, but I need a comma first –* (pause while the students write down the appropriate punctuation) *'Do you want to come to the cinema with me this evening'.* (pause again) *And I mustn't forget the question mark.* In this case, the students would

each write down: *Karima asked Nobuko, 'Do you want to come to the cinema with me this evening?'* Encourage the students to help each other as they write.

4 When you have finished, ask the students to form small groups to check that they agree about what they should have written down. If necessary, put your version on the board.

Variation

If you think the students would have difficulty following the instructions at Step 3, write up on the board what you expect them to write during your think-aloud phase. After this first demonstration, ask two more students to hold a conversation. This time do the activity without the demonstration.

Focus on script

When each student has completed their writing, ask them to form groups of 7–8 and take turns at flashing – showing their writing to the rest of the group so fast that the other students barely have time to see it and take in its overall structure. When everyone has flashed, each group should decide which students appear to have done the writing task properly. This is not as difficult as it may sound: because there are two speakers taking four turns, there should be four separate paragraphs. But don't tell the students this, let them guess it. This is a script exercise to the extent that it requires recognition of script layout.

2.4 Using typographical conventions – designing a handbill
Level 3↑

Time   40 minutes, plus homework

Materials   Texts (see *Preparation*)

Process stage   Editing: improving layout

Preparation

Choose two texts such as a handbill advertising a service, film or event, or a ticket for the cinema, train, bus, etc., or an advertisement.

For elementary students, use two texts of the same type; for intermediate students you can use different text types. Photocopy one of them and prepare and copy a plain text version of another from which all distinct fonts, colours and other design features have been removed. Samples are provided at the end of the activity if you want to use these.

Procedure

1 Distribute copies of the handbill. Ask the students to work in small groups and identify the various typographical conventions and work out why they are used.
2 While the groups are in discussion, note down on one side of the board (or OHT) typographical conventions such as capitals, italics, boxes, illustrations, etc. found in the handbill.
3 Take each convention and discuss its uses.
4 Give the students the prepared plain text and ask them to redesign it as a homework task, making use of as many conventions as they think appropriate. The results make an interesting wall display.

Follow-up

If there is an opportunity to advertise an event in your school, get your students to make an advert using the typographical conventions you have worked on in class.

Variation

Begin by brainstorming everything that a take-away pizzeria would want to put on its handbill or a theatre manager on a theatre ticket and then ask groups of students to work on the design of the handbill or ticket.

Focus on script

Ask the students to reflect on the ways in which the script they used for this activity differs from that which they would use for everyday writing. Discuss the variations in script in various kinds of everyday writing – this will involve discussion of size and neatness at least.

```
The Hong Kong Polytechnic University
Peter Grundy
Associate Professor
Department of English
Hung Hom, Kowloon, Hong Kong
Tel: (852) 2766 7555
Fax: (853) 2333 6569
E-mail: eggrundy@polyu.edu.hk
Flat 06, Pak Tak Yuen, 2 Lok Kwai Path, Fotan,
Shatin, N.T.
Tel: (852) 2688 6244
```

The Hong Kong Polytechnic University

Peter Grundy
ASSOCIATE PROFESSOR
Department of English

Hung Hom, Kowloon, Hong Kong
Tel: (852) 2766 7555   Fax: (853) 2333 6569   E-mail: eggrundy@polyu.edu.hk
Flat 06, Pak Tak Yuen, 2 Lok Kwai Path, Fotan, Shatin, N.T.
Tel: (852) 2688 6244

```
mistletoe pizzeria
18a mistletoe road  jesmond
tel   212 3333   212 1232   212 0150
[map: acorn road osborne road mistletoe road we are here]
open every night 5.00 pm till late
free drink with every pizza order over £3.60
free delivery on orders over £6.50
limited delivery area and minimum order of £4.00
80p charge on all other deliveries
home cooked pizza delivered to your door
happy  hours  15%  off  any  order  to  collect  or  deliver
between 5-6.30pm sun-thurs
students 50p off at all times on counter collection only
10% off for party order over £30
```

2.5 Listing

Level 3↑

Time   40 minutes

Process stage   Drafting

Rationale

The purpose of this activity is to enable the students to write a fully punctuated text about a topic of interest to themselves with an appropriate specialist vocabulary.

Procedure

1 Write up a list of topics on the board which are likely to be of interest to the students in your class. Suitable topics might include *keeping fit, cooking, preparing to go out on Friday night, becoming rich, making friends, driving.* Ask for further suggestions from the students and continue until every student in the class can find at

least one topic in the list which they are interested in. Ask the students to form groups with other students interested in the same or a similar topic.

2 Each group then writes a single sentence on a piece of paper in the form *We would like to be better at* … , followed by their own topic.

3 They then pass the paper to the next group who write *Then you need* … followed by a list of all the things they need to do. Remind the students that each item in the list will also need to be separated by a comma, except for the last item which will be preceded by *and*. So if one group writes *We would like to be better at English*, the reply might be something like *Then you need to work hard, listen to tapes, watch English language television, learn more vocabulary and find a friend who speaks the language.*

4 When the answers are complete, they are returned to the original groups. Because the topic is their special interest, they will very likely wish to add items to the list before copying out and reading the sentence aloud to the class for possible further comment.

Variations

i This can also be done as a mime activity. Pair two groups: each takes turns at miming what they would like to be better at, and the group watching the mime then writes down the activity. You may need to help with the vocabulary. Mime requires group decision-making and helps to draw attention to detail – for example, miming being better at English would reveal some of what's involved in being good at English.

ii You can also make this a shopping list activity. The response takes the form *Then you need to buy* … .

iii Or a descriptive activity. For instance, if a student writes *I am interested in athletics*, the other members of their group can write a response for them in the form *At an athletics meeting, participants* … .

iv Other topics with list-making possibilities include occupations (e.g. those involved in horse racing or the tourist industry), houses (furniture), newspapers (sections).

Comment

This draws on the interests and expertise of the students, but presents them with problems of finding English vocabulary for areas of interest where their basic vocabulary will be that of the first language. It therefore prepares them to write and talk more easily in English about their interests.

Focus on script

Some of the letters in the Roman alphabet can be formed in more than one way. When the lists are returned to the original groups, they will have five or six different students' handwriting on them. Ask the group to look for any differences in the way the different writers have formed the following letters: *b*, *d*, *f*, *g*, *p*, *q*, *s*, *y*. Does each writer always form each of these letters in the same way? Ask the students to try forming these letters in the way that other students have chosen, and to decide whether they want to continue forming letters in their own original way or are considering changing their handwriting.

2.6   **Making labels**   Level 2↑

> **Time**   40 minutes
>
> **Materials**   Preferably, address labels or gummed paper to cut into label-sized pieces; otherwise small pieces of paper and glue
>
> **Process stage**   Targeting

Rationale

The purpose of this activity is to encourage the clearest possible handwriting so that on those occasions, such as form-filling, when the students need to write uniform, non-cursive script, they do it well.

Procedure

Each student should think of a real-world situation in which they are required to write really clearly. Possible situations might include writing to an elderly friend or relative with poor eyesight, writing a greetings card, writing the gift-tag for a present, writing a message that includes foreign words or proper names unknown to the reader, writing a letter of application for a job, etc. Suggest they think of situations in which they use labels – luggage labels, labelling jars or bottles, labelling files, etc. Distribute labels and ask each student to write two such labels in English, paying special attention to script, which should be non-cursive (i.e. each letter is written separately), with the letters as uniformly spaced as possible and properly positioned on the label. Encourage the use of bilingual dictionaries where necessary.

Follow-up

You can move on to more creative labelling, for example, students can create designer labelling for clothes, or even an appropriate label for each item of clothing they are wearing at the time.

Variations

Try to think of other occasions on which really neat handwriting is required and devise simple activities based on such situations. For instance, the students can think of the last occasion when they were required to write really neatly in their own language and reproduce this in English. Or they can design invitations or write messages in cards. Or they can fill in an important form as neatly and accurately as possible. Some examples are given.

Please send:
□ 12 Mixed Carnations £11.25 **£9.25**
□ 18 Mixed Carnations £14.50 **£12.50**
□ 24 Mixed Carnations £17.25 **£15.25**
□ 20 Mixed Freesias £11.75 **£9.75**
□ 10 Mixed Roses £14.75 **£12.75**
□ 12 Carnations & 20 Freesias (mixed) £18.25 **£16.25**

Offer Valid until 31st Oct. 1998

□ Tick to receive FREE colour brochure.

Prices include postage and packaging to the UK. Please allow 3 working days from receipt of order.

PLEASE PRINT CLEARLY IN CAPITALS
To: Mr/Mrs/Miss _____
Address: _____
_____ Postcode: _____
Sender: Mr/Mrs/Miss _____
Address: _____
_____ Postcode: _____ Tel: _____
Message (12 words max. or enclose own card):

Payment: I enclose £_____ cheque/postal order payable to
Guernsey Fresh Flowers or charge £_____ to my
□ Access □ Visa □ Diners □ American Express

Card No ☐☐☐☐☐☐☐☐☐☐☐☐☐☐☐☐ Expiry Date ☐☐☐☐

Date flowers to arrive by
/ /

Card Holder Signature _____

Send with remittance to:
Guernsey Fresh Flowers (Dept. IW 2/98), La Couture Road, Guernsey, Channel Islands GY1 2EA.
Tel: 01481 716599 / 722280 • Fax: 01481 714656
From time to time we may pass your name and address to other companies who we believe offer products in which you may be interested. If you wish to avoid this please write to us at the above address.

ROYAL MAIL STAMP COLLECTORS CLUB
APPLICATION FORM

Just send a crossed cheque or postal order for the appropriate
amount made payable to: 'Royal Mail Stamp Collectors Club'.
Please do not send cash or stamps.

INDIVIDUAL MEMBERSHIP

Name _____

Address _____

_____

_____ Postcode _____

Country _____

Date of birth _____

Telephone number _____ Sex: Male ❑ Female ❑

Signature of parent/guardian (if under 18) _____

❑ I enclose £5.00 for 2 years' UK membership
❑ I enclose £7.00 for 5 years' UK membership

OVERSEAS MEMBERSHIP

❑ I enclose £9.50 for 2 years' membership
❑ I enclose £13.50 for 5 years' membership

GROUP MEMBERSHIP
(10 or more members: £3.50 each for 2 years,
£5.00 each for 5 years)

Group Name _____

Name of Group Leader _____

Address of Group _____

_____

_____

Postcode _____ Number of members _____

I/we enclose £   for ❑ 2
❑ 5 years' UK membership (please tick).

Focus on script

Ask each student to write their label out again in the kind of everyday script they would use when writing a letter to a friend. Ask them to consider the ways in which this script is more economical than the formal script they worked on in the activity.

2.7 Spelling with a difference
Level 3↑

Time Steps 2–4: 15 minutes

Materials Drafts of student writing

Process stage Editing

Rationale

Although students are encouraged to try to spell as accurately as possible, with lots of words it's genuinely difficult for them to know whether they have succeeded or not.

Procedure

1 Next time your students are doing a piece of individual writing, instruct them that whenever they are unsure of the spelling of a word, they should make sure they misspell it. Moreover, they should misspell it in a way obvious enough for their colleagues to recognise the misspelling and at the same time still know what word is intended. They should also write as neatly as possible so that their misspellings can be read without difficulty.

2 When the writing is complete, each piece of writing should be passed to the student sitting on the writer's left. Each student now underlines all the misspellings they can find. Again, the writing is passed one place to the left.

3 Each student now attempts to write in correct spellings wherever there is an underlined word. Again the writing is passed one place to the left.

4 Repeat Step 3 three more times. Each time, the students should write in their suggestions for the misspelt words, <u>even if they are writing in the same suggestions as have been made by a previous student</u>.

5 When the pieces of writing reach their original authors, the authors should check that the 'corrections' are in fact correct. Encourage the use of dictionaries at this stage. Any remaining doubts should be referred to the teacher before the corrections are studied and committed to memory.

Variations

i Step 1 can be a homework as well as an in-class activity.

ii The misspellings produced in Step 1 can be visually signalled too, for example by underlining or using a different coloured ink.

Comments

1 This is a fun activity which often gets the students talking among themselves about spelling in English. The peer-correction element is very satisfying for the students – and for the teacher.

2 Although we agree that incorrect forms should not in principle be supplied to learners, we think that this activity is justified because a clearly incorrect form is preferable to the covertly incorrect one the students would otherwise produce.

Focus on script

Being able to spell accurately is partly a matter of being able to recognise that the word you have written looks right. At Step 4, tell the students that when they are writing in a correct spelling already suggested by a previous student, they should imitate the handwriting of that first student and then write the word in their own natural handwriting in their rough books. Do both versions look equally correct?

2.8 Consequences – story writing   Level 4↑

Time   30–40 minutes

Materials   Small sheets of blank paper

Process stage   Drafting: punctuating quotations

Rationale

The combination of creativity and humour in the controlled framework of the well-known party game of Consequences allows for repetitive practice of sentence and quotation conventions.

Procedure

1 Divide the class into groups of seven. Supply each student with a separate small sheet of paper. Stress the need for good handwriting and punctuation as the most interesting story will go up on the wall. Explain that each story will be seven sentences long with a different student writing each sentence. There will be two characters – a man and a woman who are well-known and have been in the news. Explain that each student writes a sentence and passes the paper to their neighbour, who writes the next sentence.

2 Each story begins in a particular place. Dictate *This story took place ... .* Explain that the place can be anywhere, such as *in the Albert Hall in London* or *at the airport in Hong Kong*. After each student has completed the sentence starter in their own way, ask them to pass their paper on to the person sitting on their left, who should check to see that the spelling and punctuation are correct.

3 The next sentence mentions the weather. Dictate *It was a ... .* The students complete with expressions such as *dark and stormy afternoon* or *bright, sunny morning*, and pass the story to the person sitting on their left.

4 The next line starts *On one side there was ... .* This should be followed by the name of and something about a well-known man, such as *Ronaldo, the Brazilian footballer* or *Bill Gates, with his credit card.*

5 The next line begins *Nearby was ...* and is followed by the name and description of a well-known woman, such as *Martina Hingis with her tennis racket* or *the Chinese actor, Gong Li.*

6 The next line starts *He said to her, '...'* and finishes with something like '*Are you enjoying it here?*' or '*What a funny place to meet!*'

7 The following line starts *She replied to him, '...'* and finishes with something like '*Not with you around.*' or '*Yes, isn't it?*'

8 Finally, the story ends *The consequence was ...* and ends with something like *they never spoke to each other again.* or *they decided to meet more often.*

9 The group then reads all the completed stories and selects two for you to choose from to display using the criteria of accuracy of punctuation and interest.

Variations

You may choose a different framework as long as it is a clear one. The examples can be simplified for beginners. The role of male and female can be reversed. The activity can be written with the paper being folded over after each sentence so that the next writer doesn't know what has gone before. The advantage of this is that it is more humorous. The disadvantage is that it can easily lead to careless punctuation and to incoherent stories.

Comment

Guided writing of this kind gives a sense of confidence to students as they move towards freer writing where they are responsible for both content and form.

Focus on script

You can ask the students to use different scripts (e.g. with and without serifs [see examples on the next page], or cursive and non-cursive, or large and small, or upper and lower case) for the part you dictate and the part they write. Sensitising students to script in this way can help to raise their awareness of the options they also have. This is important since virtually all users of Roman script mix serif and non-serif, cursive and non-cursive, and, necessarily, upper and lower case.

Script with serifs:

This is what the doctor meant
This is what the doctor meant
This is what the doctor meant

This is what the doctor meant
This is what the doctor meant

Script without serifs:

This is what the doctor meant

2.9   Punctuation templates   Level 4↑

Time   60 minutes

Materials   Punctuation templates (see *Preparation*)

Process stage   Drafting

Preparation

Either prepare two punctuation templates of your own or make use of those provided below (which are taken from texts that appear in *Headway Elementary*):

Template A: Cap , . Cap , , . Cap , . Cap . Cap , , . Cap , .
Template B: Cap ? Cap . Cap , . Cap . Cap – , , , , , . Cap . Cap .

The advantage of making up your own lists is that you can choose texts the students have just read and make punctuation lists from those. At the end of the activity, this enables the students to compare their own writing with the texts from which your punctuation lists were made.

Procedure

1 Either wait till you next ask your students to write a formal text or agree a topic with them for them to write about now. Good topics for this activity include descriptions of places they know well, suggestions for how to enjoy a holiday or a Saturday night, or predictions for the world/their work/their company/their friends over the next year. If you are working with a coursebook-derived template, the topic of the coursebook text is ideal. If you have

quotation marks in your punctuation template, the topic you choose will need to be one that allows the students to use dialogue.

2 Ask each student to consider carefully just what they want to say. If it helps, allow them to make notes.

3 Once they know what they want to write, instruct them to choose either punctuation list A or B, and do their writing in such a way as to use the punctuation in the order specified in the list.

4 When the students finish writing, it's worth discussing any difficulties they encountered. Because this activity shows how punctuation orchestrates our writing, in the discussion you should have a better opportunity than usual to make the point that punctuation really matters.

Variation

Rather than have a template in the form of a list, you can prepare a punctuation sheet. It's best to use lined paper for this. Copy the specimen sheet below if this is useful. The students then write in such a way as to complete the punctuation sheet by filling up the spaces between points of punctuation with as many words as they want. Because you have specified the distance between punctuation points, this is a harder task.

Punctuation sheet
(_ indicates that a capital letter is required here.)

_————————————————— , ———————————
———————— . _————— , ——————————— , ———
———————————— . _———————————
—————————— , ——————————— . _———
—————————— . _———
————————— , ——————————————
————————— , ——————————————
———————— . _——————————
——————— , ———————————
——————————— .

© Cambridge University Press 1998

Focus on script

Ask the students to pay special attention to the difference between the capitals and the regular letters and to circle all the capitals which are not formed in the same way as the corresponding regular letters. You can also ask the students to check that the relationship of punctuation marks to their written text is consistent and conventional.

3   Confidence building

The activities in this section are simplified versions of real-world writing which will give your students a sense of achievement and confidence in their ability to do 'real' writing. The activities are ordered so that those that are least demanding come first and the more challenging activities come later. You will notice that sometimes the students work on everyday types of writing and sometimes on more specialist, or even exotic, types.

3.1   Shopping for a friend – *aide mémoire*   Level 2↑

Time   40 minutes

Materials   Pictures of different kinds of uncooked foods as you would find them in the shops, market or supermarket (optional)

Process stage   Planning

Rationale

Making lists is one of the commonest uses of writing in the real world, either as an aid to memory or as preparation for further writing. It provides practice of a kind of stress-free writing whose form comes naturally.

Procedure

1 This step is optional. Describe one of your favourite dishes to the class. Ask the students to consider what they would need to buy to cook this dish for you and list their suggestions on the board. You'll find this is much easier if you have pictures of food to show.
2 Pair the students and ask them to discuss some of their eating preferences. Then get each student to write down their favourite dish at the top of a piece of paper. You may have to help with

vocabulary – in an English-speaking country this will have a lot of face validity as your students will be keen to learn restaurant English.

3 Each student then exchanges their paper and writes down a shopping list of what would be needed to make their partner's dish. They can ask the partner as many questions as they like about the ingredients that would be required. Bilingual dictionaries are often useful at this stage.

4 If there is time, pairs can be invited to talk over their preferences and the lists with another pair or to make a wall display.

Variations

i You may build into the lesson a simulated shopping expedition for which the list would have to be more precise. For instance, instead of *bread*, *a small loaf of brown bread* would be substituted, instead of *eggs*, *half a dozen eggs*, etc.

ii With more advanced classes, pairs can decide on a whole meal.

3.2 Writing instructions

Level 2↑

Time 25–30 minutes

Process stage Drafting

Procedure

1 Ask each student to write down three instructions that could be carried out in the classroom by another member of the class. The person to be instructed should not be identified at this stage. Possible instructions might include:
– Please lend me your pen.
– Please let me see your book.
– Please stand up.
Give help where necessary and check that the instructions have been written down accurately.

2 Ask for a volunteer to start the process. He or she selects a fellow student and reads out an instruction. When the instruction has been performed, the performer then selects the next student and reads out an instruction. Continue in this way. Explain that:
– If a student doesn't understand an instruction, they must carry out whatever instruction they guess they are being given. If the

performance indicates that they haven't understood, another student should be selected.

– If one of a student's instructions has already been used by a previous student, one of their other instructions should be used.

3 You may sometimes want to have a pause between instructions so that members of the class can write the instruction down, together with a sketch of the performance to enable them to remember the meaning.

Variation

For intermediate students you can work with requests that exhibit 'negative' politeness forms such as **Could** I *borrow your pen* **for a moment, please?** and **Would you mind if** I *had a* **quick** *look at your book?* (Brown and Levinson [1978, 1987] distinguish 'positive' politeness in which speakers show interest in and approval of those they talk to, and 'negative' politeness in which speakers show how they respect each other's rights or territory.)

3.3 Writing about food

Level 3↑

Time   35–40 minutes

Process stages   Drafting; evaluating

Rationale

The aim of this activity is to build confidence by limiting writing to simple sentences from which the best examples are selected and read aloud.

Procedure

1 Ask each student to write four sentences about food. Two of these should be short sentences of six words or less, and two should be longer – of seven words or more. Stress that the sentences can be about typical menus, likes and dislikes, where food comes from, etc. If food isn't an ideal topic, choose another one.

2 Ask each student to exchange their list with the person sitting next to them. Each student chooses the more interesting short sentence and the more interesting long sentence from their partner's list to read aloud to the class. Allow time for discussion of each set of sentences.

Follow-up

A subsequent lesson can draw on the same topic to produce a connected piece of writing of 6–8 sentences, or may use some or all of the random sentences produced previously in a more logical order with the right connecting words. Breaking a complex task up into two stages in this way also enables you to talk to your students about the composing process.

3.4   **The perfect instruction**   Level 4↑

Time   30–35 minutes

Process stages   Planning; drafting

Procedure

Ask the students to write down the instructions they would like to leave their families if they were going to be away for a week. Before the students start to write, it may help to brainstorm the areas which their instructions might relate to – how their pets/children or car/adults should be looked after in their absence, what their families should repair or repaint or replace while they are away, what 'welcome home' celebrations their families should plan for them, what overdue bills their families should pay for them, what areas they hope to receive good news in when they return. Make time for the students to show each other their work or talk about it to the class, explaining the reasons for their instructions.

Variations

i   You can specify other formats besides a list of instructions. For example, the instructions can take the form of a timetable.

ii   The instructions can be directed at a particular family member and be supported by instructions to another family member to monitor the way the first family member carries them out.

iii   Explanations as to how to carry out the instruction can be added in later.

iv   Other variations include writing instructions to yourself when you're going to be away, and instructions to a person at work or in one's family who's going to be away.

3.5 Representing self – personal writing   Level 5↑

Time   45 minutes

Process stages   Targeting; drafting

Procedure

1 Divide the class into groups of 4–5. Choose a topic, in this case school experiences (but see *Variation* for other suggestions). Put a number of sentence starters on the board, such as:

> One of my earliest memories is …
> My happiest memory of school is …
> The funniest thing that happened at school was …
> The worst thing that happened at school was …
> We laughed a lot when …
> Our teacher got really angry when …

2 Explain that each student should choose two of the starters and write two sentences using each of them – one must be true of themselves and one untrue.
3 The sentences are read out in the group by the person to the left of the writer; group members have to guess which sentence is true and which untrue.

Variation

The sentence starters can be in any relevant or interesting field such as families, leisure activities, careers, talents, interests or friends.

Acknowledgement

Paul Davis and Mario Rinvolucri suggest a simplified form of this activity in *The Confidence Book*.

3.6   **Simplifying writing**   Level 5↑

Time   40 minutes

Materials   Any text that can be simplified for a different readership

Process stage   Rewriting

Preparation

If you have a coursebook with texts, you can choose a suitable text from it. Otherwise a short newspaper item or encyclopedia entry works well – make one copy for every pair of students.

Procedure

1 Divide the class into pairs. Distribute the text and explain that you want the students to provide a simpler version for a readership less familiar with English. If they can write for the class at the level below them, this gives them a sense of what is required. Or if you are working with a quality newspaper text, you might ask the students to write a popular newspaper version. (If you have such a version yourself, comparing the students' and the authentic texts makes a good follow-up activity.)
2 When the writing is complete, make time to discuss the issues that arise.

Variations

i   You can ask your students to bring a piece of fairly technical writing on a topic that interests them and simplify it for someone who knows much less about the topic.
ii   Another variation is to provide a colloquial piece of writing and ask your students to make it more formal.
iii Or you can make this a translation activity from the mother tongue into English.

Comment

Some of your students will go on to use English in the workplace and may well find themselves required from time to time to take a professional text and produce a lay version of it for a less expert readership. This kind of activity is a good first exercise in this kind of work.

3.7 Writing instructions to accompany a picture sequence
Level 5↑

Time 40 minutes

Materials A picture sequence, such as the vacuum cleaner one given on the opposite page

Process stages Drafting; editing

Procedure

1 Distribute the picture sequence and ask the students to write a set of instructions to accompany the pictures. As they finish writing, encourage them to compare what they have written with their neighbours.

2 Ask for a volunteer to write their suggested text on the board and invite comments on it. It usually works best to keep the volunteer at the front of the class so that they can amend their instructions if they are persuaded by what their classmates suggest. If necessary, guide the discussion to the most important issues, which include:

   – whether to use more formal (Romance) or less formal (Germanic) vocabulary (e.g. *extract* versus *pull out* for the second picture in the sequence supplied);
   – whether to use definite articles or not (e.g. *pull out bag* versus *pull out the bag*), and how consistent to be about this;
   – how much work to leave to the pictures and how much to let the words do. You can also discuss how the instructions would be different if there were no accompanying picture sequence.

Comment

This activity appears quite easy to do, but the discussion stage reveals how much can be learnt about this sort of writing and that the choices facing the writer are much more extensive than they might at first appear to be.

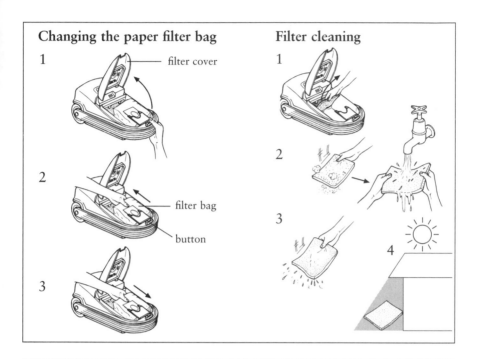

Changing the paper filter bag

1   filter cover

2   filter bag

    button

3

Filter cleaning

1

2

3

4

3.8   Glossing a text – personalising text   Level 5↑

Time   40 minutes

Materials   Text; dictionary; if possible, OHT
(see *Preparation*)

Process stage   Editing

Rationale

The purpose of this activity is to build on the skills your students already have by asking them to gloss words they don't understand in texts. They are also encouraged to write their reactions to what they read in the text too.

Preparation

1 Choose a text of 3–4 sentences which is linguistically challenging and has an interesting content. The coursebook for the next level up may be a good source of suitable texts. If you have an OHP, you can copy the text onto an OHT, although this is not necessary.

2 Make a photocopy of a second triple-spaced text of comparable difficulty and interest for each student. Two examples are given below.

WHY DO CONTACT LENSES MAKE SENSE?

Contact lenses let you look at life in a new way. Suddenly you'll have all-round vision again. There will be no more misting-up when you walk into a warm room. You'll see clearly in the rain. Enjoy sport with greater freedom. Show off your eyes like you once did. And, best of all, no one need ever realize that you are wearing them.

If you are receiving malicious telephone calls, we at BT want to help. Whether the calls are obscene, threatening or just a plain nuisance we are committed to working with you to tackle the problem.

1 Remain calm. Try not to encourage the caller with an emotional response; and remember it's your telephone and you are in control.
2 Do not enter into any conversation. Simply place the handset down beside the telephone and ignore it for a few minutes before replacing it gently.
3 If the caller phones repeatedly, don't say anything when you pick up the handset; a genuine caller will speak first.
4 If the calls are silent, don't attempt to coax the caller into speaking; just replace the handset gently if no one speaks.
5 Don't ever give out any details about yourself or your family unless you are absolutely sure you know and trust the caller.

Procedure

1 Write the first text up on the board. Or if you have made an OHT, display it. Allow the students a few moments to decide on and indicate any difficulties they have in the text. With their help, gloss the difficult words or phrases in a second colour chalk/whiteboard pen. If you're using an OHP, it's a good idea to use an overlay for this procedure and for Step 2.
2 Discuss the content of the passage with the students and summarise their questions and comments using a third colour. Finally, your text might look something like this:

---

are   *worth buying*
WHY DO CONTACT LENSES MAKE SENSE?
plastic lenses fitted to the eye-ball ⟨what a claim!⟩
   Contact lenses let you look at life in a new way. Suddenly you'll
⟨only by turning your head⟩   *moisture on the lenses*
have all-round vision again. There will be no more misting-up when
                    ⟨agreed⟩
you walk into a warm room. You'll see clearly in the rain. Enjoy
⟨only if you don't drop your lenses!⟩ *exhibit proudly*
sport with greater freedom. Show off your eyes like you once did.
       ⟨but what about designer glasses?⟩
And, best of all, no one need ever realize that you are wearing

them.

---

3 After the students have understood the possibilities available when
   glossing a text, give them a copy of the photocopied text to gloss
   themselves. Encourage the use of dictionaries.
4 When the task is complete, they can compare their results with
   those of another member of the class before you hold a brief class
   discussion. Alternatively, you can make a wall display of the glossed
   texts.

Variation

If you have an OHP, you can prepare the two overlays before the start
of the lesson. This enables you to discuss them with the class rather
than elicit students' response to the text from cold.

Comments

This work is loosely related to advanced note-taking. Make sure your
students are warned against writing in valuable books! The advantage
of using coursebook texts is that this activity will make the texts more
comprehensible and more relevant to the students.

3.9 Recording telephone messages   Level 6↑

    Time 40 minutes

    Process stage Drafting

Rationale

This activity bridges the gap between spoken and written skills and
prepares the students for real-life situations.

Procedure

1 Describe the following typical situation: you telephone a hotel to make arrangements with a resident, but the resident is out so you have to leave a message. Ask the class to brainstorm other situations in which you might call someone and find them out so have to leave a message for them. List these situations on the board in the form *I call a business colleague who has gone out for a meal so I leave a message with the hotel receptionist; I call the electrician but he is on call so I leave a message with his wife; I call my classmate but she has gone to the cinema so I leave a message with her mother; I call my cousin but she is visiting a friend so I leave a message with her father; I call the garage but the service manager isn't available so I leave a message with the receptionist; I call my teacher but he has gone shopping so I leave a message with his wife,* etc.

2 Ask each student to choose one of the situations listed on the board. They should decide on the reason for their call and write down the message they are going to leave if the person they are calling is out.

3 Each student should find a partner who has chosen a different situation from themselves. Join in yourself if there are uneven numbers. Explain that each student will make the call to their partner, who will take on the role of the person receiving the call, i.e. *hotel receptionist, electrician's wife, classmate's mother,* etc. The caller must dictate the message and their partner must make sure that it is accurately recorded, so may ask for repetition, how to spell names, etc. Explain that the message will need to be taken down in the third person even though it will be dictated in the first person.

4 Ask the students to sit back-to-back and make their calls.

5 When both students have made their calls, they should each compare their message with the version their partner wrote down, note any discrepancies and try to work out why they occurred.

Variation

You can ask your students to decide on the message they would leave in English on their telephone answering machines if they were out. This should be written down prior to being recorded.

Comment

One of the skills being developed is for the listener to find ways of interrupting the speaker to clarify words, meanings and spellings. It is often helpful to discuss which techniques worked well after they have been used successfully.

3.10 Writing a weather forecast   Level 6↑

Time   40 minutes

Materials   Weather forecasts from British papers

Process stage   Drafting

Preparation

Make one copy of a local weather forecast from your country's English-language newspaper for each pair of students in the class. There is an example on the next page.

Procedure

1 Divide the class into pairs and give each pair a copy of the weather forecast. Draw attention to the technical vocabulary indicated in the key.
2 Each pair should then write a forecast for the weather seven days from today (i.e. if today is Monday, they write a forecast for Monday of next week).
3 When the writing is completed, allow time for pairs to compare their forecasts.

Follow-up

At the same time the following week, you can ask the students to make any changes to bring their forecasts into line with the actual weather.

Variation

If the weather in your country is very settled or predictable, you may want to adapt this activity by asking your students to write long-range forecasts for the next two or three months.

Comment

You might want to tell your students that in Britain the weather is a safe topic which people often use at the start of a conversation. This is because British weather is very variable, very local and very unpredictable, and so there's always something interesting to say about it.

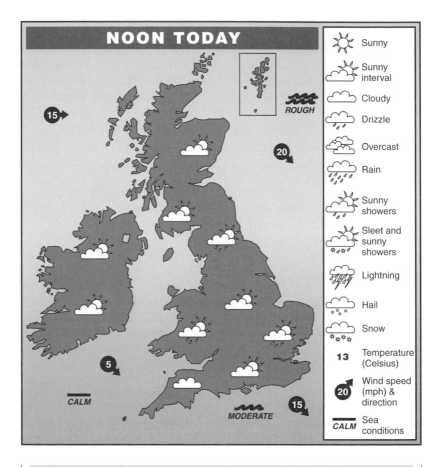

FORECAST

☐ **General:** England and Wales should see any showers dying out from the west as the morning goes on. Most places will then have a dry day with sunny spells, but cloud will increase from the west later. It will be warm, with the northwesterly breeze dying down.

Scotland and Northern Ireland should be mostly dry with sunny spells. Northeastern parts of Scotland will have showers or some longer spells of rain for a time. It will be breezy at first.

☐ **London, SE England, E Anglia, E England, NE England:** showers dying out, then dry with sunny spells. Wind northwesterly, fresh, moderating. Max 17C (63F).

☐ **Central S England, E Midlands, W Midlands, Channel Isles, NW England, Lake District and Central N England:** generally dry with clear or sunny spells. Wind northwesterly, moderate to fresh. Max 16C (61F).

☐ **SW England, S Wales, N Wales, Isle of Man, and N Ireland:** dry at first with sunny spells, becoming cloudy with drizzle later. Wind west or northwest, mainly moderate. Max 14C–16C (57F–61F).

☐ **Borders, Edinburgh & Dundee, SW Scotland, Glasgow, Central Highlands, Argyll, and NW Scotland:** showers dying out, then dry with clear or sunny spells. Wind northwesterly, moderate to fresh. Max 13C (55F).

☐ **Aberdeen, Moray Firth, NE Scotland, Orkney, and Shetland:** mostly cloudy with showers or longer spells of rain. Wind westerly, moderate to fresh. Max 10C–12C (50F–54F).

☐ **Outlook:** cloudy and damp in the west, the east dry with sunny spells.

3.11 Creating characters – descriptions of people

Level 6↑

Time 60 minutes

Materials A4 paper; eight labelled boxes

Process stages Organising; drafting

Preparation

You will need eight cardboard boxes – the boxes photocopying paper comes in are good. Label each with one of the topics that you are going to dictate to the students (see *Procedure*).

Procedure

1 Distribute a sheet of A4 paper to each student and ask them to tear it into eight slips. Explain that each student should write one fact about themselves on each slip as you dictate the topic. Because there are eight slips, there will be eight topics. They should not put their names on these slips. Tell them that the first topic is *What I look like* and that they have a minute to write clearly and honestly about themselves.
2 Dictate the remaining topics at one-minute intervals. You can invent your own list, ask your students for suggestions, or use those suggested below.

> – What I like doing
> – What I like watching/listening to
> – What I hate doing
> – What I hate having to watch/listen to
> – What I hope for in the future
> – What annoys me about myself
> – What annoys me about others

3 When the eight slips have been completed, each should be put in the appropriately labelled box.
4 Ask the students to take one slip from each box and then study the character they have in front of them carefully. They should give the person a name (but not the name of anyone in the class) and write

a description of the person using all the facts in front of them. Encourage them to try to make the person as alive and convincing as possible.

5 Share the results by having some of the descriptions read out or by putting them on the wall.

Comment

If you feel happy about participating yourself, it adds an important extra dimension. Students will find that having the descriptions in front of them removes the difficulty of not knowing what to write about, even though the mixture may at times be bizarre.

4   Focusing on process

Most of the processes involved in writing run in parallel so that treating them as stages, as we do here, is something of an idealisation. Nevertheless, it's true that most of the planning occurs early in the writing process and most of the rewriting occurs late. Thus the activities in this section are arranged according to the 'stage' at which they are most crucial in the writing process.

4.1   Planning with rods – making essay plans
Level 4↑

Time   40 minutes

Materials   Set of Cuisenaire rods or several sets of felt pens; blu-tack

Process stage   Planning

Rationale

The aim of this activity is to explore possible ways of structuring essays so that student writers become aware of the range of structures available when organising the content of a piece of writing.

Preparation

1   You can use sets of felt pens if you don't have Cuisenaire rods. Or you can make sets of strips of coloured card. You may need five sets of different coloured pens or strips of card. (See Steps 1 and 4 in *Procedure* below.)
2   You will need to decide in advance on a topic for the students to write about. Good general topics include leisure, weekends, families, modern lifestyle, home.

Procedure

1 Explain that the class is going to plan an essay. Write the topic, for example, *Holidays*, in the middle of the board. Ask the students to brainstorm sub-topics that they might expect to cover in their essay. Write each major sub-topic on the board so that you end up with a board diagram, like this:

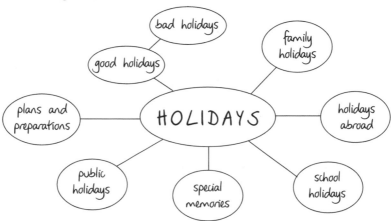

Make sure that there are no fewer than five and no more than seven sub-topics.

2 This is an optional stage which helps the students to think more deeply about the topic: invite the students to think of as many questions as possible about the sub-topics. Write these questions on the board next to the appropriate sub-topic. After 5–10 minutes, the class may wish to modify the sub-topics.

3 Choose as many different coloured Cuisenaire rods as there are sub-topics and blu-tack each rod to the board next to a sub-topic.

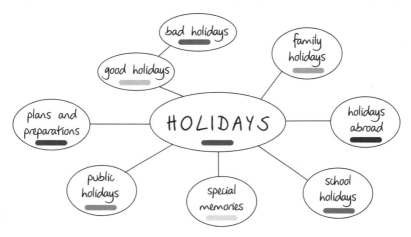

From now onwards, each rod represents the sub-topic next to which it is fixed.

4 Divide your students into groups – five in a group is a good number, although the activity will work with larger groups. (With one set of Cuisenaire rods you cannot have more than five groups since there are only six rods in some colours.) Ask the groups to plan the structure of their essay with the rods. Explain that the rods should be arranged on their desks so as to show the linear development of the essay. The rods may be placed diagonally, horizontally or vertically and may even stand upright. Rods may touch or be arranged apart. They may be placed on top of one another. Allow ten minutes for this stage.

5 Allow time for the students to circulate and look at the essay plans made by other groups.

6 Hold a discussion with the class in which you discuss the various options for organising content that the different groups have decided on.

Follow-up

You can ask the students to convert the essay plans in rod form into a written essay plan, or even to write the essays.

Variation

This activity works especially well with ESP or EAP classes because you can choose a topic from the students' professional field about which they already know a great deal. It also has face validity if you choose a topic that students are being asked to write about in their business or academic life outside the classroom.

Comment

Manipulating the rods makes it much easier to experiment with different possible essay plans. It also enables different students to make suggestions by moving rods and talking as they do so. In addition, when all the groups have finished their plans, the students can see at a glance how the different essays are structured. You will often find groups who use a vertical axis for a major sub-topic and a horizontal axis for minor sub-topics contained within the major one. This means that the students have begun to hierarchise their information without your explicit instruction. If you are a bit doubtful about trying this activity, we suggest you spend 5–10 minutes setting up the figure in Step 3 and then trying Step 4 for yourself. We guarantee that you'll see essay structures you could never have imagined otherwise which are made possible by the different arrangements of the rods (or pens or coloured card).

....

4.2 Planning writing
Level 6↑

Time   25–30 minutes

Materials   A set of notes or comments about writing
(see *Preparation*)

Process stages   Planning; organising

....

Rationale

The purpose of this activity is to get the students to reflect on the planning stage of the composing process by evaluating statements about writing and writers and ordering them in an essay plan.

Preparation

Prepare a list of about ten statements about writing for your students to consider. You can choose statements from the list on the opposite page if you like. Either make a copy for each student or write the statements on the board (before class if possible) or put them on an OHT.

Procedure

1 Allow the students to work individually or in pairs. Explain that you will be giving them a set of statements about writing and that they should decide which 5–6 they would use in an essay about writing. Explain that the purpose of the lesson is to work out the essay plan which will revolve around these 5–6 statements. The essay plan should be written down in note form and will include sub-topics suggested by the chosen statements as well as suggestions for an introduction and conclusion. If you have made copies of the statements about writing, distribute them; otherwise write them on the board at this stage if you didn't get a chance to do it before the lesson started, or put the OHT up on the screen.

- The better we become at writing, the harder it gets/the longer it takes.
- Everyone can learn to be a good writer.
- Good writers are good re-writers.
- If we know what we want to say and who we are writing for, everything else will take care of itself.
- If we use a word-processor, we will do most of the revision of our writing as we write.
- In a hundred years' time, no one will write any more.
- It doesn't matter if no one wants to read what we write.
- It's better to start writing without wasting a lot of time thinking first.
- Most writing is informal.
- The pen is mightier than the sword.
- Practised writers revise after they have finished writing, not during their writing.
- Readers are more powerful than writers.
- Spelling doesn't matter in English.
- Think before you write, not while you write.
- Word-processors help us to be better writers.
- Writing is a written record of speech.
- Writing is much easier if we plan everything carefully and make detailed notes before we start.

© Cambridge University Press 1998

2 Once the students have made plans, ask them to get together in small groups to discuss these plans. If time allows, ask some of the groups to report back to the class.

Follow-up

You can always ask the students to write the essays they had planned. These make a nice wall display if set out around the original set of statements.

Variation

There is no need to use statements about writing when asking students to make an essay plan, although it makes sense to do this when you are focusing on writing itself. If you decide to ask the students to make essay plans from your own initial statements on some other topic, make sure that the statements reflect a variety of positions. You can also brainstorm the statements with your class.

4.3 Knowing your reader – writing advertising copy Level 3↑

Time   30 minutes

Process stage   Targeting

Rationale

Advertisements are a good way of drawing attention to the importance of the reader, because the audience is the prime concern of the copywriter.

Procedure

1 Ask the students to work in small groups. Each group is going to design an advertisement, and so first they need to decide on the product they wish to sell. It may help if the class brainstorms possible products or if you bring in pictures of products or even products themselves.

2 When each group has decided on a product, ask the groups to think about the person to whom they hope to sell it. It sometimes helps to agree on a few things: for example, the target buyer will be someone who doesn't presently own the product; the more target buyers that can be identified the better – so the description will need to be general as well as specific, etc.

3 When each group has decided on their target buyer, each member of the group should draw a picture of this target buyer.

4 Finally, each member of the group thinks up their own original one-sentence slogan or sales pitch to write somewhere on the sheet on which the target buyer is depicted.

5 Make a wall display of the advertisements that your class have created.

4.4　**Talking to the reader**　　　　　Level 8↑

Time　30–40 minutes

Materials　One picture of a person for every pair of students (see *Preparation*); blu-tack (optional)

Process stage　Targeting

Rationale

The aim of this activity is to make the importance of the reader clear to the writer.

Preparation

Cut out at least one picture from a colour magazine for every pair of students – as many pictures as there are students is good if you can manage it. Try to choose pictures of people who look different from your students in terms of age, ethnicity, social background, etc. Although your pictures will usually be of individuals, it's also permissible to have groups provided they are all the same kinds of people, e.g. a pop group or a football team. You can also use a picture with several people in it as long as you circle the person you want your students to think about.

Procedure

1　Ask the students to work in pairs. One student is going to be the writer and the other is going to take notes on what goes on while their partner writes. Once each pair have decided who is to write, the writer should choose a picture from the set you have brought to class. This picture represents the person they are going to be writing for.

2　Once they have chosen a picture, each pair should spend two or three minutes working out a few imaginary biographical details of this reader. After they have done this, ask them to choose a topic to write about which their reader can be assumed not to know much about. Before starting to write, the writer should display the picture of the reader in front of him/her. If your classroom is big enough for everyone to sit facing a wall, the pictures can be blu-tacked to the walls. The note-taker should sit either beside the writer or, when possible, at right-angles to the writer and the reader's picture.

3 Explain that the writers should try to talk to their readers as continuously as possible throughout the writing period. They should explain to the reader, using their mother tongue if they wish, why they are writing and planning to write as they are. The note-taker should record as much of the commentary as possible, again in the mother tongue. Allow 20 minutes for the writing phase.
4 Allow a few minutes for the pairs to discuss how the running commentary directed at the reader altered the writing. Let them talk together before asking for whole-class comments.

Follow-up

One optional follow-up activity is to ask the students to display their writing around the classroom walls. Shuffle the pictures of the readers so that each pair has a new picture and ask them to blu-tack it under the writing they think was directed to the reader whose picture they now have. This is a fun activity – do not expect accurate guesses unless you have a small class and very different pictures.

Variations

i If your students have cassette recorders, they can practise this technique by themselves at home. You can also ask each student to bring their tape to class and be ready to talk about one interesting moment in it. This variation obviously works well in one-to-one teaching or for small-group work.
ii Another option is to work with groups of three and have the third student imagine they are the person in the picture. This means that

the third student will describe who they are, where they live, their family status, occupation, interests, etc. before the writing starts. They may also comment on whether they like the way they are being written for while the writing progresses. This variation is more suited to adults – it often works better if you allow the third student to use their mother tongue.

iii If you want all your students to have the experience of writing and of note-taking, you can repeat this activity with the roles reversed, although usually the lesson is well learnt by both students whichever role they are in.

Comment

Many of us are too lazy to think very hard about the people who are going to read what we have written. This activity demonstrates how very great the influence of a reader can be when the writer keeps their reader constantly in mind.

4.5 Arranging yesterday's diary   Level 5↑

Time   50–60 minutes

Materials   Felt pens (optional)

Process stage   Organising

Rationale

Very often the so-called 'writer's block' occurs because we don't know where to start or in what order to arrange our ideas. In this activity, the students work with a chronological outline and then organise the content of their writing by picking out what is exceptional from this given material.

Procedure

1 Ask each student to take a sheet of paper and write yesterday's date at the top. Do the same thing yourself on the board.
2 Explain that everyone is going to fill in the events of the day hour-by-hour in diary form. Ask each student to write the hour when they woke up in the margin at the top of the page and the hour when they fell asleep in the margin at the bottom of the page. Do the same thing yourself on the board.

3 Ask the students to write down an hour-by-hour account of what they did between the time they woke up in the morning and the time they fell asleep at night. Do the same thing yourself on the board. As the students will inevitably read your diary while they write, set a good example by being fairly detailed. For example:

> 7   woke up
> 7–8   got up, showered and shaved, dressed – put on my new shirt, listened to the radio – heard my team had won their match
> 8–9   had breakfast, picked up my post – a big bill I wasn't expecting so soon, walked to work
> 9–10   my first class

It's a good idea to get the students to work in pairs and to discuss any points of interest or difficulty with each other as each works on their own diary.

4 When a good number of students have finished, introduce the idea of organisation by eliciting from them that time order is the organising principle and that within that ordering the day could, in addition, be divided into morning, afternoon, and evening.

5 Discuss the fact that some events will happen regularly on most days while others are more unusual. For example, in the list on the board, listening to the radio may be a daily occurrence, whereas the team will only win from time to time. Ask the students to highlight the more unusual items in their diaries with an exclamation mark (!) and the more regular items with an asterisk (*). Alternatively, you can use different coloured felt pens for this step and Step 6.

6 Some events are less pleasant than others. Ask the students to mark the less pleasant events in their diaries with a minus sign (–) and the more pleasant with a plus sign (+).

7 If you have a small class, divide it into two groups. One group makes lists of regular and more unusual happenings based on their diaries. The other makes lists of unpleasant and pleasant events. This works nicely if you ask the students to work together in two groups and then use the board to display their findings. If you have a large class, ask the students to work in groups of 4–6.

Follow-ups

1 It's possible to move on to simple connected writing such as: *Yesterday was in some ways like any other day. I woke up at seven*

o'clock, got up, showered, shaved and had my breakfast ... (this includes asterisked items), followed by a second paragraph, *Some happenings were less predictable. For instance, I heard on the radio that my team won their match. I also got an unexpected bill through the post. We had a new teacher at nine o'clock* ... and a third paragraph, *Every day has pleasant and unpleasant events. I was pleased that my team had won, but the big bill spoilt the morning* ... . It may be helpful to supply the first sentences for each of these paragraphs.

2 You might want to use this activity to raise your students' awareness of the fact that we need criteria for organising longer pieces of writing and, as this activity shows, chronology isn't always the best or most pertinent criterion.

Variation

Your class can brainstorm other ways of distinguishing events, such as solitary versus communal activities, or those which involve talk and those which don't. Or groups can brainstorm and then make the teacher a present of the best idea(s) they come up with.

Comments

1 If you have access to computers and your students have word-processing skills, this activity can be done on a computer. This makes Step 7 much easier.
2 If your students are studying in an English-speaking country, this activity also prepares them for answering the inevitable questions that well-meaning native speakers put to them about what they have been doing with themselves.

4.6 Observing the writing process   Level 6↑

Time   40 minutes

Process stages   Planning; organising; drafting

Rationale

The purpose of this activity is to enable the students to find out more about how writing takes place by observing the process closely.

Procedure

1 Ask the students to work in groups – seven is an ideal number. Explain that three members of each group will be 'writers' and the other four will be 'observers'. The writers will sit in the centre of the circle and work collectively on producing a piece of writing. The observers will sit on the outside of the writers and make a collective written record of how the writers proceed. Both writing and observing groups will need to confer among themselves. The observers may ask the writers questions at any point and may look at their work in progress.
2 Ask the writing groups to work on a writing task from the coursebook. If this isn't practical, choose a task that will take a group working collectively 20–30 minutes to complete. While the writing is going on, move around the observing groups to make sure that the observers know what to do. If your students share a common mother tongue, allow conferring in their first language. You can even allow the observers to make their record in their mother tongue if you think this will help them to make a more complete record.
3 Initiate a discussion of the writing process based on the records kept by the observing group.

Variations

i You can vary this activity in several ways. For example, you can make the observers' function more proactive – they can be instructed to interrupt the writing process to conduct a more structured interview with the writers.
ii Instead of holding a class discussion at Step 3, you can arrange for each group of seven to discuss what the observers have noticed.
iii Use a camcorder to record a writing group at work – in this case you will need to edit the tape later before showing selected moments to the class as a stimulus to discussion.

Comment

Writing, like most other human activities, seems to proceed relatively intuitively. But a more conscious understanding of the processes is likely to help us to write more effectively. In addition, students very much enjoy the role of observer or bystander in classroom activities.

4.7 The school report

Level 6↑

Time 45 minutes

Process stages Targeting; organising; drafting

Rationale

This activity is most suitable for children (but also has interesting possibilities with adults – see *Variation iii*). The students are asked to think about their English and then represent their evaluation as though they were a teacher writing for their parents. This helps to promote awareness of register and audience. And if their parents understand English, this task results in a useful piece of writing to take home.

Procedure

1 Dictate a number of headings under which your students could evaluate their English. Good headings include *listening, pronunciation, writing, interest and effort, vocabulary, spelling, recent progress*.
2 Each student should make notes about their progress under each heading.
3 Explain that each student is to write a report on themselves based on these notes but written as though they were the teacher (i.e. you) writing for their parents. Remind them that reports should summarise past progress and make suggestions for areas to work on in the future. Ask them to think carefully about how to organise the material they have noted down. This can be a homework task too.
4 When the reports have been written, ask some of the students to explain how they organised the material and how writing as a teacher for their parents affected the way they wrote. If you are satisfied with the reports, you can sign them.

Variations

i The students can also write reports for other subjects (and can compare their progress in English with their progress in other subjects).

ii They can also work in pairs, with each student writing a report for their partner based on their partner's notes.
iii You can adapt this activity for adults who have an employer or sponsor who expects them to learn English and would welcome a progress report.

Comment

These reports can make a good wall display. They may also be useful if you have to write real reports and want to make them as authentic as possible.

4.8 Writing to a formula – expanding and contracting sentences
Level 3↑

Time 40 minutes

Materials A page of the class reader or any comparable piece of writing

Process stage Rewriting

Preparation

Choose a page of your class reader or other comparable text. Check the number of words in each sentence. If the second shortest sentence contains seven words, the lower word limit you set in Step 1 of the Procedure will be eight words; if the second longest sentence contains 18 words, the higher word limit you set in Step 1 of the Procedure will be 17 words, i.e. you add one to the lower number and take one away from the higher number.

Procedure

1 Allow the students to work individually or in pairs. Explain that the editor of their series of readers has decided that from now onwards there should be no sentences shorter than X words and no sentences longer than Y words. Their job is to rewrite the page taking this instruction into account.
2 When they've finished writing, give the students an opportunity to compare their work.

Variation

In this example activity we have suggested a way of making sure that each student has to rewrite two long and two short sentences. You can obviously play with the formula and set things up so that the students have to rewrite only the long or only the short sentences. And if you have a mixed ability class, you can also give different instructions to different groups.

4.9 Ways of rewriting   Level 4↑

> **Time** 60 minutes
>
> **Class size** 10–15 is ideal. Divide bigger classes into groups of this size
>
> **Process stage** Rewriting

Rationale

In the early stages of writing in a second language, many students are content simply to record information on paper. In this activity, they move on to reviewing and improving a first draft.

Procedure

1 Ask each student to think of one simple sentence that describes what they are wearing in class at present, or what they wore in class yesterday, or what they like to wear in general. When everyone has thought of a sentence, ask each student to say their sentence in turn while each member of the class writes it down. So if Naraporn says, *I wore blue jeans in class yesterday*, everyone writes down *Naraporn wore blue jeans in class yesterday*.
2 Divide the class into three groups and explain that the text created in Step 1 will be rewritten in three different ways:
   – Ask one group to make minor adjustments while retaining the original sentence order. The task is to tidy up the stylistic inelegance that results from several short sentences following each other in rapid succession.
   – Ask another group to rewrite the text radically, reordering sentences so that the text has a natural coherence. This might mean that all the sentences mentioning *jeans* or all the sentences

93

about what people wore in class yesterday were grouped together.
– Ask the last group to incorporate any new information into the text. For example, they might want to insert after *Naraporn wore blue jeans in class yesterday, but today she is wearing a red dress.*
Allow plenty of time for this task and go round helping where necessary. For example, it may help with the first group to suggest that they first try to identify four or five particularly awkward places in the text before deciding how to improve them.

3 Ask each group to read out their revised text (which make interesting reading because they are so different) and talk about the way they redrafted the original text. Comment on the underlying principles yourself.

Variations

i You can do the original writing one day and the editing another day if this fits better with the time available.
ii If you work in a school where the children wear uniform, you'll have to choose a topic like what people did after school yesterday, expect to do after school today or like to do in the evenings.

Comments

1 Notice how the topic you choose will also give practice in the use of various tenses, aspects and modals.
2 It's worth making the point that there are lots of different kinds of rewriting exercise. For example, the first group's task is a kind of deep proof-reading, in the sense that the writer is just tidying up around the edges by adding a few minor cohesive devices. The second group's task is much more radical and requires a lot of decision-making. The result is a much more coherent text. The third group's task is to add in new information – this is an important skill which is all too easily overlooked when we get to the revision stage of writing.

4.10   **Student reformulation**   Level 5↑

Time   35 minutes, or 55 minutes if the reformulating is
done in class

Materials   Photocopies of extracts from students' texts
(see *Preparation*); blu-tack

Process stage   Rewriting

The term 'reformulation' is usually used to refer to a process in which
the teacher takes a student's text and writes a parallel text which
preserves the meaning and form of the original but expresses the ideas
more accurately.

Rationale

The purpose of this activity is to help the students to discriminate
between more and less effective ways of expressing the same meaning
in a piece of writing.

Preparation

1 This activity requires a number of students in the class to volunteer
a short piece of their writing for other students to reformulate. It's
wise to obtain consent to use the students' work in this way. A
good strategy is to explain that you need a few students to
volunteer to have their writing worked on in the next lesson.
Usually students are only too pleased to have their work given such
close attention and you'll have too many volunteers!

2 Your students are going to work in groups of about eight. Each
group will need one short passage of about six lines from the
written assignment of one of their classmates to work on. (So if you
have a class of 40 students, you will need five texts.) Try to choose
passages which contain interesting ideas which could be expressed
more felicitously. Once you have selected the passages, type each
one with triple spacing and make eight copies of it (or more if your
groups are bigger than eight – see Step 1 below).

Procedure

1 Divide your class into groups of about eight. (If the class doesn't
divide equally, it's better to have bigger rather than smaller groups.)

2 Give each member of group 1 a copy of text 1, each member of group 2 text 2, etc. Ask each student to write their own reformulated version in the spaces between the lines. (This can also be a homework activity.)

3 Assign one wall, or part of one wall, of the classroom to each group and ask them to blu-tack their reformulated texts to the wall in random order. When this is done, ask each group to move one place around the classroom so that they are standing in front of a text which has been reformulated by another group.

4 Allow the students ten minutes to order the texts from most to least successful reformulation.

5 Move the groups one further place around the classroom and allow them ten minutes to decide if they want to accept or to make changes to the order decided on by the previous group.

6 You will have had time to observe closely and you will have identified the best texts for each group yourself. Spend 5–10 minutes explaining to the class where you agree and where you don't agree with their opinions.

Comment

Once a class is familiar with this activity, they will take to it readily. On each further occasion when students study reformulated texts, they will sharpen their judgement as to which reformulations are accurate representations of the meaning of the original writer.

5   A process writing project

This section continues the focus on the writing process introduced in the previous section. It consists of a series of nine activities which should be taught in a sequence. Together, they constitute a nine-lesson writing course with homework which results in a conventional product – a project which the students write largely in their own time on a topic of interest to themselves. But this is not all.

When we teach writing, we need to concentrate on raising our students' awareness of the composing process itself. For this reason, in this project, the students will not only write about a topic (such as sport or family life), they will also write about those aspects of the composing process which they experience for themselves and about the decisions they make as they write. This account of their experiences as writers appears as a series of marginal glosses alongside their project. The example below shows the second paragraph of a writing project and the accompanying marginal gloss produced by a group of students following this kind of writing course:

```
The first pair of jeans was
originated in 1853 by Levi
Strauss in the US. They are
durable, simple, functional, and
thus being worn by farmers,
goldminers, lumbermen and cowboys
in the 1850s. During that time,
jeans belonged to a product
category of work-wear.
```

The following paragraphs give the reader an overview of the evaluation and development of jeans.

We strongly recommend that you prepare a handout to guide your students through their writing course and to indicate how it will be assessed. You might want to use the following example, either as it stands or adapted to suit your own situation:

Writing course handout

1 You are starting a writing course. You will write a project on a topic to be decided in class. You will also write a commentary about your project writing – this commentary will be based on what you learn in class about writing.

2 60% of the marks will be awarded for the project you write and 40% for your commentary.

3 You may work alone, or with a partner, or in a group of three. Whether you work individually or in a group, you will submit one project. The grade will be the same for all members of your group.

4 You will need to rule a wide right-hand margin taking up approximately one-third of the page. Your project will be written on the left-hand two-thirds of the page and the right-hand margin will contain your commentary. So when you hand it in, it may look something like this:

PROJECT	COMMENTARY
Title: Life in Britain	Choosing a topic:
Authors: Denise Wah and Fiona Chan	we chose this topic
	because we have
Life in Britain is very different from	both been to
life in Hong Kong. In Britain, most people	Britain.

5 You will have some class time to write the commentary but the project itself will mostly be written in your own time as a series of homework tasks.

We suggest that this handout is distributed and explained half-way through the first activity (See **5.1 Choosing and organising a topic**, Step 4).

Homework

It works best if you allow regular homework or classroom times for the project writing, starting with the first homework after Lesson 3. We make suggestions for the stage the project writing should have reached at the end of each lesson description below. The right-hand margin description of the process should be completed in class time.

5.1 Choosing and organising a topic

Time   60 minutes (including 15 minutes explaining the
Writing course handout)

Materials   Two handouts (see *Preparation*)

Preparation

1 Prepare for the class by identifying several topics, enough for each
group of three to have a different one if possible. A good way to
choose these is to look through the coursebook for topics which
feature in it, e.g. shopping in Britain, homes in Britain, work, holidays, travel, families, conservation, youth culture, food, education,
fashion, politics, etc. If the topic is chosen from the coursebook, there
will be sources of information (see **5.4 Using sources**) available at the
right level in English.
2 Prepare copies of the Writing course handout (p. 98) and Topic
organisation handout (below) for each student.

Topic

Major area	Sub-topics	
1	a) b) c)	d) e)
2	a) b) c)	d) e)
3	a) b) c)	d) e)
4	a) b) c)	d) e)
5	a) b) c)	d) e)

© Cambridge University Press 1998

Procedure

1 Write the topics on the board. Ask the students to group themselves in threes and then choose a topic. If it's possible for each group to have a different topic, this is good.
2 Ask each group to brainstorm around the topic and make a web diagram like the one below. This could easily be made by students working with many of the coursebooks published in Britain:

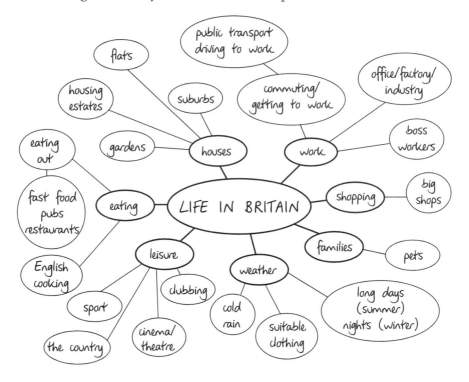

3 Ask the groups to sort their diagrams out into 4–5 major areas which they expect to write about, and arrange these so that sub-topics are detailed too. So for *Life in Britain*, the areas might be families, homes, work, leisure, positive and negative features. Distribute copies of the Topic handout to help the groups do this.
4 So far your students have been working in groups of three. At this stage they should decide whether to continue to work as a group, or to work as a pair and an individual or as three individuals. Before they decide this, distribute the Writing course handout and work through it making sure that everyone understands what they will be required to do. Allow the students a few minutes to decide whether to continue as a group or to split up.

5 Tell the students (groups, pairs, individuals) to rule a wide right-hand margin and write the heading *Choosing/Organising a topic* in it at the top, and then add a sentence or two of their own describing how they chose their topic and made their plan. Help with the English if necessary.

6 Finally, the students should write the title of their topic (e.g. *Life in Britain*) and the names of the author/s at the top of the left-hand portion of the first page opposite the heading *Choosing/Organising a topic*.

5.2 Identifying the reader

Time 35 minutes

Procedure

1 Explain that you are going to dictate a series of questions about who the students are writing for. Explain that you will pause for two or three minutes after each question while they make some decisions and note down what they agreed. These questions will help them identify their target reader/s. Good questions to dictate include:

> – Are your typical readers native speakers of English or not? If not, what is your readers' mother tongue and level of English?
> – How old are your readers? Are they male and/or female?
> – What occupations do your readers have? Do they like their work?
> – How do your readers spend their leisure time? What sort of television programmes do they like? What sort of newspapers do they read? How would a typical reader spend the weekend?
> – Why do your readers want to read about the topic you are writing about? What do they already know about the topic?

2 Ask the students to imagine one single reader of what they are going to write. They should note down their imaginary reader's name, age, sex, occupation and reason for reading.

3 Ask the students to write in the right-hand margin under *Choosing a topic*, the heading *Identifying a reader*, and then to add a sentence or two of their own describing their readership. Help with the English if necessary.

5.3　Writing the opening paragraph

Time　30 minutes

Procedure

1 Ask the students to brainstorm all the things they would expect to find in the opening paragraph of a piece of writing. Write their suggestions up on the board. Obvious things you expect to hear include *what the writing is about and who it is for, why the topic is important or relevant, how the writing will be organised, what position the author(s) will take, how the reader's initial interest will be aroused, how the reader's continuing interest will be maintained.*
2 Ask the students to write in the right-hand margin under *Identifying a reader* the heading *Writing the first paragraph* and then to add a sentence or two of their own describing what a first paragraph should contain. Help with the English if necessary.
3 Tell the students, who now know their topic and their readership, to plan the first paragraph of their project, which will be written in the left-hand two-thirds of the page.

Homework/Project work

Actually writing the first paragraph makes a good homework activity. The students should then work on the next two or three paragraphs of their project so that they have made some progress by the time they come to the next writing class.

5.4　Using sources

Time　55 minutes

Procedure

1 Explain that you are going to dictate a word every minute for ten minutes. The students should treat the words as prompts and write whatever they are stimulated to write about for as many or as few of these words as they want to – so if they are still busy writing about the first word when you dictate the second, there's no need for them to write about the second. Explain that the average student will probably write something about three or four of the words. Dictate

whatever words you like – here are some suggestions: *clothes, illness, weekends, love, money, property, kindness, colour, rain, summer, food, faces, computers, feelings, night-time, streets, buses, football, music.*

2 At the end of the ten minutes, ask the students to put their writing aside, and begin a new piece of writing on another sheet of paper. This should begin with the sentence, *People are very different from each other*, should contain two more sentences of the students' own invention, and end with the words *For example ...* , which will be the opening words of a fourth sentence which will be written later.

People are very different from each other. Some differences are natural – sex, age, etc. Some are personal. For example ...

Note: it will help when you get to Step 6 below, if you have done the same writing task as your students. You can probably complete Steps 1 and 2 in the time you allow your students for Step 2.

3 Explain that the sentence beginning *For example ...* and the one that follows it (i.e. the fourth and fifth sentences of their writing) will draw on what classmates wrote in response to the earlier dictation.

4 Ask the students to display their prompted writing on their desks. Allow ten minutes for everyone to move around the classroom look-ing for information from this prompted writing to incorporate into their own *People are very different* piece of writing. As they move around, they should note down anything they wish to quote or refer to, along with the name of the original writer.

5 After ten minutes, ask the students to go back to their own desks and complete the *For example ...* sentence and write one further sentence in which they refer to the source material they have just been study-ing. Explain that anything they quote directly from their classmates' writing should appear in quotation marks. These quotations, as well as any paraphrases in their own words, should always indicate the original source, e.g. (Perez 1999).

6 The students should also write a sixth, concluding sentence that is all their own. If you are also doing the writing task, write your version up on the board during this time.

7 Spend a few minutes drawing out the principles of working with sources – you can use your own writing to illustrate a) the value of using sources, and b) the standard way of acknowledging them.

8 Ask the students to turn to their projects. Tell them to choose a place in the right-hand margin opposite the place in their project where they expect to use a source (such as their coursebook). The students should use what they have learnt in class to write two or three sen-tences about the use of sources under the heading *Using sources*. Help with the English if necessary.

Homework/Project work

The students should continue their project out of class, making sure that they use and acknowledge one or more original sources. They should be encouraged to review earlier work to see whether it contains claims which would benefit from supporting evidence – if so, they should seek out sources. Supply examples of bibliographic referencing so that they see how to cite references in their text and how to list them at the end. You can use our examples on page 185 if you like.

5.5.1 Writing exactly

Time 40 minutes

Materials Slips of paper with symbols (see *Preparation*)

Rationale

The purpose of this activity is to help the students to think carefully about just how to express their meaning now that they are in the middle of writing their project.

Preparation

Prepare one set of six slips of paper for every four students in the class. Each of the six slips in a set should have one of the following symbols written on it.

$	%	→
♪	☺	TM

© Cambridge University Press 1998

Procedure

1 Ask the students to form groups of four. Distribute a set of slips of paper to each group. Each group should think out a simple story, two or three sentences long, which uses as many as possible of the symbols as prompts. For example, a group might decide that someone was listening to music and smiling because they had just become very

rich, etc. As each group agrees its story, each individual member of the group should begin to write it down in their own way without consulting their fellow group members.

2 Allow ten minutes' writing time for each member of each group to produce their own version of the agreed story. Encourage the students to think carefully about exactly how they want to express their meaning.

3 Allow a further ten minutes for each group to evaluate the completed stories and then to join with another group to exchange information about the options each writer in the two groups exercised. For example, if one student has written *She listened to the music and smiled – she would never be poor again* and another has written *The music was good. She thought of all her money, and laughed*, the groups might want to decide which of these two versions captures the original idea more exactly or whether neither is as good as some other student's version.

4 Ask the students to leave their groups and turn to their projects. The students go to the place in the right-hand margin opposite the point they have reached in their project so far. The students should use what they have learnt from this lesson to write two or three sentences about expressing exactly the meaning they have in mind, under the heading *Expressing meaning exactly*. Make the point that this lesson has not been about correctness so much as about conveying an agreed meaning as exactly as possible. Help with the English if necessary.

Homework/Project work

Ask the students to keep the idea of exactness in mind in any project work they do before the next lesson and to review earlier work with exactness as well as accuracy in mind.

5.5.2   Organising material

> **Time**   30 minutes
>
> **Material**   Stories written in 5.5.1

This lesson should follow on directly from **5.5.1 Writing exactly**.

Procedure

1 Ask the students to work in groups of eight which are made up, if at all possible, so that no student is working with anyone they had

worked with in the previous activity. Each student should read all the stories the members of their new group had written in the previous lesson. The group should then decide on three categories so that each of their eight stories falls into one of the three. For example, one category might be stories with happy endings, another might be stories in which someone sang, another might be stories involving a journey.

2 When each group has come to a final decision, the group should talk through the process by which they determined the categories and distributed the stories among them and then write a simple paragraph describing this process. Collect in the paragraphs – you will need them for the following activity, **Linking paragraphs**.

3 Ask the students to turn to their projects and decide on the place in the right-hand margin opposite the place at which they feel that their project shows evidence of being an organised piece of writing. They should use what they have learnt about organisation to write two or three sentences under the heading *Organising ideas* which will help them to organise the rest of their project as effectively as possible. Help with the English if necessary.

Homework/Project work

The project should be nearing completion now. Encourage the students to review the organisation of ideas in their earlier work.

5.5.3 Linking paragraphs

Time   45 minutes

Preparation

Before this lesson you will need to make photocopies of the paragraphs that you had collected from the previous activity. Make one copy of each paragraph for every four students in your class.

Procedure

1 Ask the students to work in groups of four. Distribute a complete set of paragraphs to each group. Explain that each group should decide which four paragraphs they want to work with.

2 Once each group has chosen their four paragraphs, explain that these should be arranged in order, with the paragraph describing the agree-

ment that was reached most easily first, and the paragraph describing the agreement that was hardest to reach last.

3 Explain that you want each group to write five single sentences or short phrases which will bind the four separate paragraphs together into a coherent piece of writing. The first sentence should introduce the writing and will be placed before the first paragraph. A sentence or phrase will occur before each of paragraphs 2, 3 and 4 to link each paragraph to the one before. The fifth sentence will occur after the fourth paragraph and will conclude the piece of writing.

4 Ask the students to display their writing on the wall. Allow them ten minutes to read the work displayed on the walls and note down any useful ways of linking paragraphs which they notice in their class-mates' writing.

5 Ask the students to turn to their projects and find the place in the right-hand margin opposite the first place in their project where they feel that two paragraphs are particularly well linked. They should use what they have learnt about linking paragraphs to write two or three sentences under the heading *Linking paragraphs* which will help them to link the paragraphs in the rest of their project as effectively as possible. Help with the English if necessary.

Homework/Project work

The students should review the way their paragraphs are linked throughout their project. The first draft of the project should be completed by the next lesson.

5.6 Checking and rewriting

Time 45 minutes

Materials Coloured dots or felt pens

Procedure

1 Ask your students to brainstorm as many reasons as they can think of for checking original writing and, where necessary, rewriting it. Stress that the focus of the brainstorm should be on why we need to rewrite rather than on what we do when we rewrite. It's best if the students work in pairs or small groups first and then you can write up on the board all the ideas the groups provide. Be ready to supplement their reasons with your own. Try to write the reasons up on the

board so that they are ordered from micro to macro reasons. Reasons for rewriting include:
- to check spelling
- to check punctuation
- to check grammar
- to improve expression
- to identify sentences that simply feel wrong
- to identify sentences that are too long or too short
- to identify sentences where the meaning is unclear
- to look for places where the expression could be more economical
- to make sure that there are enough paragraphs
- to check that the paragraphs are in the right order
- to find or think of relevant new information after writing the first draft
- to check that we remembered who we were writing for throughout our writing

2 Allocate one or two reasons to each pair/group and ask the group to make a list of the kinds of things they should typically do when rewriting. So if, for example, a group was allocated to check punctuation, the kinds of things they would list would include inserting full stops where they had been overlooked, making sure that questions had question marks, considering places where colons or semi-colons might be effective, considering whether any colons or semi-colons they had used were really necessary, etc.

3 Ask the students to display on the wall the reasons for rewriting and the typical strategies they use when rewriting.

4 Give each student a set of red, a set of green and a set of blue coloured dots of the kind used for colour coding books in school libraries. (Alternatively, they can use red, green and blue felt pens.) Ask the students to circulate, reading each of the wall displays and adding a red dot if they think this rewriting strategy should be applied only at the end of each page of writing, a green dot if they think it should be applied only at the end of the entire piece of writing, and a blue dot if they think it should be applied at the end of each page and again at the end of the entire piece of writing.

5 Ask the students to turn to their project and go, first, to the bottom of the right-hand margin on the first page and write two or three sentences about continuous checking of writing under the heading *Checking writing*. Next, they should write two or three sentences about appropriate strategies for rewriting in the right-hand margin under the heading *Rewriting* and opposite the point where they expect their project to be completed, if it isn't already completed.

Homework/Project work

The groups should be using their out-of-class time to check their projects carefully and rewrite where necessary.

5.7 Linking process and project

Time 30–40 minutes

Procedure

When your students have completed their project, they will have a written text in the left-hand two-thirds of the page and a series of comments about the writing process in the right-hand margin. Ask the students to work through their project adding a sentence or two to each place where there is a right-hand margin comment about the writing process. These additional sentences should indicate how they actually went about the process stages they have written about while working on their project. Because your instructions at the end of the first two lessons, but not after that, more or less told them to do this, they will probably only need to add comments from *Writing the first paragraph* onwards.

6 Computers and writing

The activities in this section range from those which can be done without the use of computers (although computers make them easier) to those which require a word-processing program and even, in some cases, e-mail. Because word-processing programs allow a wide range of formatting possibilities and make editing and rewriting much easier, they are of obvious use in teaching writing. E-mail allows your students to communicate rapidly with each other and to share writing-in-progress. For each activity we indicate which facility is required. The activities are arranged so that those that involve the least complicated operation are at the beginning of the chapter and those that involve more complicated operations are at the end.

In the case of e-mail activities where each member of the class needs to be able to communicate with their fellow students, each student will need an e-mail address. They will also need to make an address folder or file, so that any message they send goes to everyone in the class, including yourself. You will probably have to show them how to do this and may even have to learn how to do it yourself first. The immense sense of achievement mastering e-mail gives can be glimpsed from this first message sent by a student one of us taught after she had successfully made an address file:

```
My dear classmates,

Wow! it's really hard to create the file. It takes me
quite a long time but I finally made it! I will send a
mail to you very soon as now I still don't know what
to say as I am so happy!

Sara
```

Sara was a member of a class in which the students agreed to communicate with each other about their language learning by e-mail.

In a situation like this, you can ask different small groups of students to take special responsibility for each week of the term and to ensure that the class e-mail network is full of interesting messages and questions. As an assignment, each group can be asked to make a folder of the e-mail messages from their week and to add some further comments of their own.

If you don't have access to computers, you might like to think about how some of the following activities can be done using conventional means. In fact, it may be useful to begin by looking at the very first activity.

6.1 Guest authors – imitating a style   Level 5↑

Time   Ten minutes within a longer piece of writing

Computer function   Word-processing – also possible without computers

Process stage   Drafting

Rationale

In this activity, one student writes part of the composition of a fellow student. The aim is to make the students aware of the style, plot and characterisation of a fellow student's writing.

Procedure

When your students have made some progress on a piece of writing which they are doing on their computers, either individually or in a group, ask them to exchange computers with another individual or group. Allow ten minutes for the students to guest-author the next stage in the writing before asking them to return to their own computers to finish their work. Do not tell them that you are going to ask them to take over each other's writing until the moment when you want them to swap computers.

Follow-up

There are several nice follow-ups to this activity. Simply discussing what each group would have written next if the other group hadn't hijacked their work is fun, as is discussing the problems and opportunities provided by the guest-authoring.

Comment

You don't need a computer for this activity. But it's more fun this way, and when the writing is printed out, no one can tell from its appearance which part was written by one author and which part by another. In fact, it makes a fun guessing game for a third student or group to try to guess which part was guest-authored.

6.2   Simultaneous writing   Level 6↑

> **Time**   Not less than 30 minutes; can be ongoing
>
> **Computer function**   Word-processing – switching documents; also possible without computers
>
> **Process stage**   Drafting

Rationale

In this activity, the students work simultaneously on two texts. The purpose is to help them to plan what they are going to write carefully so that when they have to leave their current writing task, they can pick it up again later. Simultaneous chess is a good analogy. The activity works best if you have enough computers for each student to work alone, but it can also work well with groups.

Procedure

1 Explain that the class will have 30 minutes to complete two pieces of writing and that they should work on the first topic until you tell them to switch to the second. Explain that you will instruct them to switch between topics at frequent intervals. Assign the first topic and ask the students to get to work on it.
2 After 3–4 minutes, ask the students to switch to a new document. Assign the second topic and tell the students to get to work on it.
3 Ask the students to switch between documents at random intervals. Make sure you advise them when they are switching to a document for the last time.

4 When the time is up, the students will probably want to talk about their writing and about the extent to which one piece of writing influenced the other. Try to guide the discussion around to the importance of planning writing and yet at the same time being open to the new changes of direction that seem appropriate as we write.

Variation

Instead of giving switch commands, give a general instruction such as: *You have to produce two pieces of writing and will be expected to switch between each at least three times during the 30 minutes you are allowed – you can decide when to switch.*

6.3 Correcting texts – suggesting improvements in writing
Level 4↑

Time   15–20 minutes

Computer function   Word-processing – deleting and inserting; emboldening

Process stages   Drafting; editing

Rationale

Word-processing makes improvement/correction much easier than formerly and also has the advantage that a corrected text does not show any evidence of an original, less accomplished version. Although this is one of the most obvious uses of computers in teaching writing, this doesn't make it any less valuable.

Procedure

1 While your students are in the drafting phase of their writing, ask them to stop work and make a copy of what they've done. They then switch computers and improve/correct each other's work. As there is a back-up copy, they can make changes to the text they see on the screen.
2 The students return to their own computers, and compare the changed text with their original.
3 Allow a few minutes for discussion between writers and correctors.

Variations

i The corrections can also be made as suggestions in brackets (more trouble but it enables the original writers to decide whether or not to accept the suggestions).

ii It's also possible to ask the students merely to highlight things that they would change and leave it to the original authors to act on these hints. The best way to do this is to ask the students to change anything they have doubts about to bold or italics.

Comment

When texts are written in longhand, it's usually possible to tell whether we are reading a draft or a final version. With word-processed texts, this is not usually possible provided that a spell-check has been used. Since each person's handwriting is different, most texts feel close to their authors, especially in classrooms where students recognise each other's handwriting. Because word-processed texts do not reveal the author in the same way and are taken by default to be final versions, they seem to be objectified and to invite a more critical, outsider's reading. Thus they are more correctible as the product of someone else's industry than handwritten texts are.

6.4   Handwriting and word-processing   Level 2↑

[cap]**T**[c]**ime**[tab][tab][tab]**30**[space]**minutes**[hrt]

[cap]**M**[c]**aterials**[tab][indent][cap]**A**[c]**ny**[space]**piece**[space]of[space]**writing**[space]**recently**[srt] **completed**[space]**by**[space]**the**[space]**students**[hrt]

[cap]**C**[c]**omputing**[space]**function**[tab][cap]**WP**[c][hrt]

[cap]**P**[c]**rocess**[space]**stage**[tab][cap]**D**[c]**rafting**[hrt][hrt]

[cap]**R**[c]**ationale**[hrt]

[cap]**T**[c]**his**[space]**activity**[space]**gives**[space]**the**[space]**students**[space]**the**[space]**opportunity**[srt] **to**[space]**complete**[space]**a**[space]**writing**[space]**task**[space]**successfully**[space]**just**[space]**by**[srt] **being**[space]**really**[space]**careful.**[hrt][hrt]

[cap]**P**[c]**rocedure**[hrt]

[cap]**A**[c]**sk**[space]**the**[space]**students**[space]**to**[space]**take**[space]**a**[space]**short**[space]**piece**[space]of[srt] **their**[space]**recent**[space]**writing**[space]**and**[space]**copy**[space]**it**[space]**out**[space]**with**[space]**word** [hyphen][srt]**processing**[space]**codes**[space]**inserted.**[hrt][hrt]

6.5 Slimming down – producing an economical text
Level 3↑

Time   20–30 minutes

Materials   A text

Computer function   Word-processing – deleting; also possible without computers

Process stage   Editing

Rationale

In this activity the students delete redundant words. Making the judgement about whether the writer has used just the right number of words or whether the writing could be more effective if it were more economical requires real skill. Yet the exercise isn't difficult to do and the resulting text, in which the student has done no more than delete, is, in a sense, the student's own writing. Deletion is also fun and usually makes students feel good.

Preparation

Select a text and make it available on disk to each student or group. If you have networked computers, you can send it to each student/group as an e-mail message. You need an interesting text at the right level for your students from which words can be deleted to leave a modified text which still makes sense. If you have a reader or a coursebook with texts in it, you may find something suitable there. Or you can copy one of the texts on the next page.

Procedure

1 If everyone has a computer, the students should work individually. Otherwise, divide the class into as many groups as you have computers.
2 Explain that the students should delete any words which can be removed and still leave a meaningful text. It's usually a good idea to illustrate with an example.
3 Ask the groups to compare their results before having a whole-class discussion about the effects of deleting items.

I think that Christmas is a very different time from any other time that I can think of. For a start, no one at all, except for those that really have to, would even dream of going to work. Secondly, it's the only time nowadays when families really get together. Thirdly, children really enjoy it and so create a good atmosphere for everyone, adults included. Even when children no longer believe in Father Christmas, they still manage to pretend that there just might be such a person. It's probably the only thing that children don't want to grow out of. Although it's fashionable to grumble about Christmas and say that it's just a time of commercial exploitation, in their heart of hearts, most people really like it, even if it was always much better when they were young, of course.

If you have never seen snow, you may know what it looks like from the pictures you've seen, but you probably can't begin to imagine what it feels like. First, when it's actually snowing, the air feels kind of thick and, in a strange way, not as cold as you'd expect. The snow itself soon turns wet if a flake lands on your face or head – it goes from a white flake to an icy globule of water which fails to run off you as you'd expect. But snow is most interesting of all when it's lying on the ground. Sometimes it's dry and powdery and, try as you may, you just can't get it to hold together in a ball. Sometimes it's firm and has just enough moisture in it to make a really good snowball – the only thing better than a snowball is throwing it at someone. And sometimes, it's just wet and slushy, so that if you tried to make a snowball from it, you'd just find yourself holding a handful of slush – something between water and snow, a kind of icy, wet mass.

It's interesting to think of some of the technology that I use every day now and which didn't exist not that many years ago really when I was a child. The most obvious thing to me is the computer – I live with a computer, at work and at home. In fact, at home we have three computers and I somehow manage to find a different use for each. And then, there's the self-service petrol pump and the hole-in-the-wall ATM at the bank. I can remember when both of these seemed really new ideas and many people would admit that they were frightened of using them. And I remember when our neighbours got their first television and I used to go to their house to watch the flickering black-and-white screen which seemed to show nothing but cowboy films. And in those days, we didn't even have a fridge, and so the milk used to go sour in the summer. And every year we all got excited because yet another new artificial fibre had been invented and our clothes would apparently wash better and last longer.

Variations

i   There are many possible variations. For example, you can ask your students to delete only redundant adjectives or adverbs.

ii You can allow only a set number of deletions and ask the students to decide which of the candidate items they would delete and why.

iii More ambitiously, you can ask the students to delete not redundant items, but items which wouldn't be true for their experience in, for example, a description of a typical weekend or a journey to work.

iv Set a word limit to which the text has to be reduced. If you use this variation, check to make sure that it can be done without having to rewrite or reorganise the original text.

6.6   **Expressing a viewpoint**   Level 7↑

Time   30–40 minutes

Materials   A text

Computer function   Word-processing – deleting and inserting

Process stage   Rewriting

Rationale

Word-processors give us the freedom to experiment with a text without making a mess. This means that we can make both minor changes and quite major ones without having to retype or rewrite the entire text.

Preparation

Choose a base text with which to work. The following text works well, although you may have to explain that on St Valentine's Day people send anonymous 'Valentine' cards to people they find attractive.

Two people who travel to work on the same train fall in love with each other. They have never spoken. Neither knows for sure that the other person loves them. Just before St Valentine's Day, she decides to buy him a card and hand it over before she gets off the train on St Valentine's Day. She buys the card. She is ready to hand it over, but just before she does, he gives her a card. She is too surprised to give him the one she had bought him. He has chosen the same card for her as she had chosen for him.

© Cambridge University Press 1998

Procedure

1 The students can work individually or in groups, depending on the availability of computers. Supply a text and ask the students to rewrite it as though they were present and observing the scene described.
2 It will help the students if you give an example. So, seen from an observer's point of view, the first sentence of the text in the box on the previous page might be rewritten, 'Every day I see the same two people travelling to work on my train. They keep looking at each other. I think they are in love.'
3 When the writing is completed, allow time for students to compare their results and for a class discussion of the problems and solutions that the task involves.

Variations

There are any number of variations on this theme:
i   Write the story from the viewpoint of each of the participants in it.
ii   Write the story from the viewpoint of a friend or family member of one of the participants.
iii Write the story as a projection into the future or as a past event.
iv   Write the story with added relative clauses.
v   Add an adjective to every noun.
vi   Add an adverb to every verb.
vii Write the story in a different setting.
viii Write the story so that it addresses the reader. For example, 'Imagine, dear reader, that you travel to work on the same train every morning ...'.
ix   Write the story as a parable, or moral fable, etc.

Comment

None of these are new ideas, but they are all much easier to do on a word-processor. If you ask different students to take different viewpoints, you can make a very interesting display of the results or even stage a presentation in which the same scene is looked at from several different viewpoints (along the lines of Queneau's *Exercices de Style* 1950).

6.7 Places, friends, special days – designer poems

Level 4↑

Time 10–15 minutes per topic

Materials Each student needs their own computer, so you may have to work with a group of students rather than the whole class

Computer function Word-processing – left and right justification, centring, cut-and-paste

Process stage Drafting

Rationale

The purpose of this activity is to make formal texts out of the simplest materials so that the students get a sense of achievement just from mastering a simple form.

Procedure

1 Decide on a topic, such as *A Friend*. Dictate this topic to your students, who should type it into their computers. Ask them to think of a friend, select right justification and type his or her name into the computer. The effect should look like this:

```
A friend                                    Kenneth
```

2 Keep dictating key words or phrases such as *appearance*, *dress*, *character*, which the students type flush left. Allow time in between for the students to type their description flush right, so that eventually you end up with a designer poem something like this:

```
A friend                                       Kenneth
Appearance                         A lot of black hair
Dress             Jeans, and a Cathay Pacific umbrella
Character                               Always smiling
My feeling                                  I like him
```

3 You can make this a one-off designer poem or you can go on to another topic. Suitable topics and key words that go with them include:

My home – Who lives there, My favourite room, Its smell, I'd change
My last night out – Where I went, Who I was with, What we did, It was
My job – My boss, My salary, What I like, What I don't like, My next job
My car – Colour, Age, Condition, It goes, It reminds me of
A day of the week – The morning, The afternoon, The evening, The next day
A school subject – The teacher, What we do, The best lesson, My feeling

Follow-up

Sometimes the descriptions make nice-looking poems when centred:

```
              Kenneth
          A lot of black hair
   Jeans, and a Cathay Pacific umbrella
           Always smiling
             I like him
```

Let the students try centring all the poems they have written before deciding which one to print out for a wall display.

Variations

i   Use the cut-and-paste function to move items around. For example:

```
              Kenneth
          A lot of black hair
   Jeans, and a Cathay Pacific umbrella
           Always smiling
             I like him
```

can be altered to:

```
           Always smiling
             I like him
          A lot of black hair
   Jeans, and a Cathay Pacific umbrella
              Kenneth
```

or indeed to produce lots of different poems. As well as cut-and-paste, you can encourage your students to block and copy, to produce effects like this:

```
                    Always smiling
                        Kenneth
                    Always smiling
                A lot of black hair
                    Always smiling
         Jeans, and a Cathay Pacific umbrella
                    Always smiling
                      I like him
```

ii Alter one or two words with the help of the word-processing program's Thesaurus to make a poem which makes sense but contains a new or surprising word. For example:

```
                        Kenneth
                A lot of black curls
         Jeans, and a Cathay Pacific umbrella
                    Always grinning
                      I like him
```

iii Use right-flush parentheses to make your own comments about whatever is written left-flush. For example:

```
Kenneth                          (he's Chinese, by the way)
A lot of black hair                        (I'm jealous)
Jeans, and a Cathay         (how he dresses on wet Sundays
Pacific umbrella                      in the country)
Always smiling            (he's a nice person – not because
                          life is always good to him)
I like him                          (and so would you)
```

iv Give the students a phrase or even a long word and ask them to divide it in a variety of places. For example, Wordsworth's line 'All things that love the sun are out of doors' in his poem *Resolution and Independence* allows lots of interesting realisations:

```
All                     things that love the sun are out of doors
All things that love the sun                    are out of doors
All things that love the sun are                    out of doors
All things that love the sun are out of                     doors
```

v Another technique, which we learnt from Hedy McGarrell, is to start with a word and then ask questions so that the students expand the word to a phrase, and then to a longer phrase, and then to a longer phrase again. For example, if you dictate *Friend* and then ask *What kind of friend?*, *Whose friend?* and *Doing what?*, a student might write:

```
Friend
An old friend
An old friend of my mother's
An old friend of my mother's eating an orange
```

Comment

Many of these exercises are no more than simple mechanical operations made possible by word-processing programs. But their effects in early stage writing are often dramatic and give students an immense sense of their ability to use words effectively.

6.8 Experimenting with text   Level 4↑

Time   From 20 minutes to eternity

Materials   A text

Computer function   Word-processing – find-and-replace

Process stage   Drafting and editing

Rationale

Word-processors enable us to find and replace items at the push of a couple of buttons. The results can often be dramatic and pleasing. The purpose of this activity is to make the students think hard about the effects of the texts which they have created fortuitously by this means.

Preparation

Choose a text, preferably from the coursebook, which your students can work on. Either send it to each of them as an e-mail message or allow them time to type it into their computers. If your students don't know how to find and replace items, allow time to explain the commands.

Procedure

1 The students can work individually or in small groups. Give them the text and suggest they try replacing all instances of *the* with any

items in a list of words that you can write up on the board. (Remind them to search for *the* with a space either side of it.) A possible list might be *the amazing*, *a*, *THE*, *what*, *how the*, *the main*, *flerpy* (this is a made-up word). Also allow for *the* to be replaced with nothing. This is what might happen to the text in **6.6 Expressing a viewpoint** if *the* was replaced with *the very*.

> Two people who travel to work on the very same train fall in love with each other. They have never spoken. Neither knows for sure that the very other person loves them. Just before St Valentine's Day, she decides to buy him a card and hand it over before she gets off the very train on St Valentine's Day. She buys the very card. She is ready to hand it over, but just before she does, he gives her a card. She is too surprised to give him the very one she had bought him. He has chosen the very same card for her as she had chosen for him.

2 Allow the students to choose other words to replace (*she* would be good in this text) and to choose their own words or phrases to replace them with.

Follow-up

There should be some purpose to this play. So after your students have created a few original texts, ask them to choose the best one and edit out any replacements which spoil the effect and/or grade the replacements for quality of effect. Make a wall display of the resulting texts.

Variations

i The same text can have two or more find-and-replace operations performed on it.
ii One student can suggest a replacing item to another.
iii The find-and-replace function can be used with the prompt function so that the item is only replaced if the student decides to replace it. This produces a more conventional but less thought-provoking outcome.
iv Ask the students to exchange texts and try to work out what find-and-replace operation(s) was/were performed by their partners.

Comment

This can easily become a compulsive activity because you feel that you're bound to hit the jackpot eventually.

6.9 Making macros – producing templates such as letterheads
Level 3↑

Time   20–25 minutes

Materials   Each student needs access to a computer so this may have to be a homework task (see **Procedure**, Step 2)

Computer function   Word-processing – making macros

Process stages   Planning; drafting

Rationale

This activity gives practice in producing the kind of smart letterheads and signatures (information to be added to the end of messages such as address, telephone and fax number/s) that word-processors enable us to design. Most people keep these as a macro, a program that can be run whenever we want to use the letterhead or signature.

Preparation

Make sure that you know how to make a macro as you will probably have to tell most of your students how to do this.

Procedure

1 Pair the students and explain that each will write a macro for their partner. Each student should ask their partner what they would like – memorandum template, letterhead, signature, professionally useful template (such as their equivalent of the one we are using for this book which includes Time; Materials; Process stage; Rationale; Preparation; Procedure; Follow-up; Variation; Comment).

   When students have each chosen, allow a short time for them to find out anything they need to know about their partner (such as telephone number) in order to make the macro.
2 Allow ten minutes at the screen for the students to make their partner's macro. Alternatively, if you haven't enough computers, set this as a homework task and ask them to come to class with printouts and disk versions of the macros they have made.

3 Allow time for the students to comment on the macros they have been presented with.
4 If appropriate, make comments about preferred forms for letterheads, memos, signatures, etc.

Follow-up

You can ask the students to take the macro designed for them as a first step and make any changes to it that they would want to suit their own style. If you can allow colour printing at this stage, this is usually well received and may make all the difference to a letterhead.

6.10 Planning a story   Level 7↑

> **Time** 15–20 minutes for each part of the plan; 60 minutes in total
>
> **Computer function** Word-processing – columns; also possible without computers
>
> **Process stage** Planning

Rationale

Quite often unpractised writers think that they can begin to write a story with only a very general idea of its topic and plot. The purpose of this activity is to help the students to think more carefully about their writing before they begin it.

Preparation

If your students do not know how to use the column function in their word-processing system, they must learn this first. Column work can often go wrong, so be ready to help if your students get into trouble.

Procedure

1 Assign a short story title by whatever means you usually use when thinking up titles. If you have no regular method, we suggest asking your students to spend five minutes looking through their coursebook and choosing any three consecutive words that take their fancy.
2 Tell them that they will be asked to work out a plot, a set of characters and a setting for their story, in that order. First, they

have 15–20 minutes to work out a plot, which should be presented in two columns. One column should be a paragraph describing the plot and the other a single sentence summarising it. You can exemplify with the text in **6.6**. Write up on the board:

Two people who travel to work on the same train fall in love with each other. They have never spoken. Neither knows for sure that the other person loves them. Just before St Valentine's Day, she decides to buy him a card and hand it over before she gets off the train on St Valentine's Day. She buys the card. She is ready to hand it over, but just before she does, he gives her a card. She is too surprised to give him the one she had bought him. He has chosen the same card for her as she had chosen for him.	*Plot: Man and woman fall in love on train and buy each other Valentine cards.*

3 Repeat the process either in this lesson or in a subsequent one for characterisation and setting.
4 Allow time for students to compare and talk through their ideas.

Follow-up

Your students would probably be disappointed if they didn't write their stories after putting so much effort into planning them. It's a good idea to have a story festival and set aside quite a lot of class time for reading, presenting and discussing the stories.

Variation

The columns idea is readily transferable to other writing tasks where you want a bulky text and a short summary. It is particularly favoured in instructional writing and leaflets containing public information. In ESP classes too there are likely to be many uses for this layout.

Comment

Although you can of course do this activity without a computer, it looks much better word-processed and the students take the summary-writing task more seriously.

6.11　Desktop publishing　　　　Level 4↑

Time　30 minutes

Computer function　Word-processing – creating boxes around writing

Process stage　Editing written work

Rationale

The purpose of this activity is to give writing the kind of visual impact that word-processors make possible. This highlighting should always respect the writer's meaning.

Preparation

Your students will need to know how to create boxes, shaded areas, columns and templates for this activity. They will also need to have a text to work on, either from the coursebook, or, preferably, each other's writing. Texts that work well include letters, memos, announcements, diaries – in fact all texts that are something other than straightforward pieces of continuous prose.

Procedure

1　The class can work individually or in small groups. Ask each group to choose a text written by one of the group's members and pass it on to the group sitting to their right. They should supply the text on a disk or as an e-mail message.
2　Explain that the text should be returned to the author within 20 minutes in hard-copy form if possible with significant items highlighted. The students may work with borders, underlining, shading, boxes, italics or any other feature to make the text more striking.
3　Allow a few minutes for the students to discuss the results. Make sure you draw attention to highlighting features that improve the visual impact of the text and criticise those that compromise the writer's original meaning.

Follow-up

Sometimes the original authors are eager to take their improved text away and try to do an even better job on it.

Example

It may be useful to see what Elisa's classmates did to four entries from her diary.

---

1 August

In my classroom there are ⑤ students: Annalisa, Kieran, Ishmaael, Salem and me.

| Me | Salem | Ishmaael |

| Annalisa | | Kieran |

☺ Salem is very NOISY,
but he is nice and amusing.

4 August

I visited the Minster in York and the Cathedral and castle in Durham.

☺ It was an interesting day
and I took a lot of photographs.

9 August

I think that St Mary's College food isn't so terrible, but I prefer Italian food.

☺ I like spaghetti, pizza, lasagne, etc.
☺☺☺ The Italian food is the best!

11 August

I want to ✈ to my own country.
Why?

☹ My family and pets miss me very much,
but I'm sorry because I leave my friends here.
☺ Certainly I'm going to hang their
photographs in my bedroom in Italy.

This is the text they started with:

---

1 August
In my classroom there are 5 students: Annalisa, Kieran, Ishmaael, Salem and me.
Salem is very noisy, but he is nice and amusing.

4 August
I visited the Minster in York and the Cathedral and castle in Durham.
It was an interesting day and I took a lot of photographs.

9 August
I think that St Mary's College food isn't so terrible, but I prefer Italian food.
I like spaghetti, pizza, lasagne, etc.
The Italian food is the best!

11 August
I want to come back to my own country.
Why? My family and pets miss me very much, but I'm sorry because I leave my friends here.
Certainly I'm going to hang their photographs in my bedroom in Italy.

Variations

i   A simpler version of the activity is to ask the students to use fonts alone to create effects.
ii If you are worried about using a text created by one of your students, you can use the extracts from Elisa's diary above, or even write your own diary entries.
iii You can also ask the class to design a house-style for classroom notices making use of the fonts and features that their word-processing system has.

6.12   Making templates   Level 5↑

Time   60 minutes, plus Follow-up

Computer function   Word-processing – creating boxes

Process stage   Planning

Rationale

The purpose of this activity is to create a template or outline for a fellow student to fill in. A well constructed template will not be full of gratuitous features but will be easy to write into.

129

Preparation

Make a specimen of the kind of template you have in mind so that your students can see what they might design. There is an example at the end of the activity.

Procedure

1 Divide the class into groups of 3–4 and ask each group to brainstorm as many kinds of template as they might want to devise for fellow students. Suggest possible ideas, such as diary formats, memo formats, address books. Ask one or two groups to share their thoughts. This can be done in their mother tongue.
2 Provide your own model for discussion.
3 Tell each group that they have 35 minutes to make a template for the group sitting on their right. Explain that the success of their template will be judged by how easy it is for their classmates to fill it with appropriate writing. Each group should present their template as a printout for the group for whom they had designed it.
4 Allow time for each group to clarify anything obscure in the template made for them.

Follow-up

The groups should be given the opportunity to fill the templates made for them with their own writing.

Comment

This is a challenging activity for two reasons: it requires a degree of imagination in relation to the design of a template as well as quite a lot of word-processing skill. However, in our experience many students are incredibly good at word-processing and enjoy showing their brilliance in this area.

DECEMBER 1998/ JANUARY 1999

The last week in December and the first week in January

28	MONDAY	361/4

Morning
Lunchtime
Afternoon

Evening

29	TUESDAY	362/3

Morning
Lunchtime
Afternoon

Evening

30	WEDNESDAY	363/2

Morning
Lunchtime
Afternoon

Evening

31	THURSDAY	364/1

Morning
Lunchtime
Afternoon

Evening

1	FRIDAY	1/364

Morning
Lunchtime
Afternoon

Evening

2	SATURDAY	2/363

Morning
Lunchtime
Afternoon

Evening

3	SUNDAY	3/362

Morning
Lunchtime
Afternoon

Evening

6.13   Display-messages   Level 8↑

Time   40–45 minutes

Computer function   Word-processing and e-mail

Process stages   Planning; organising

Rationale

A display-message is a message that appears on your computer screen when you access your own local network. In many institutions, display-messages are a sort of institutional diary containing important information about various departments, forthcoming events and important changes or developments. They are meant to be informative and useful.

Preparation

Check with your information officer or IT service to make sure that a display-message from your class would be acceptable. Otherwise you can make handbills to distribute in the canteen or posters to display on a notice-board. But display messages are more interesting if you can do one because they are a distinct, new genre (see *Follow-up* below). Typically you will need to have some information to give which is useful to a wide range of other members of the institution. Decide on this first – will it be about language-learning opportunities for everyone? Will it be an invitation to come and see the work of the language-teaching unit? Of the class? What will it be?

Procedure

1 Explain that the class will be writing a computer screen display-message. Tell the students the topic. Divide the class into as many groups as you have computers and allow 20 minutes for composition of the messages.
2 Get all the groups to send their drafts to each other and allow 15 minutes for each group to decide which they like the best.
3 Hold a short class discussion in which the best message is chosen and then ask each group to send an improved version to the original authoring group. The original authoring group will need to spend time out of class taking note of all the suggestions that have been made to them and producing a final draft.

Follow-up

You can encourage your students to study other display-messages on their institutional network. They tend to have a common structure which is roughly: history/background (e.g. *The Language Centre was founded in 1980 and provides teaching in ten languages to students of the University*) + information/ instruction (e.g. *The work of the English Language Teaching unit will be on open display here during the first two weeks in May*) + how to find out more (e.g. *For further information, contact the Language Centre Information Office on 2647*). Each of these three moves also has its own grammatical structures and tense forms. The result of your class study may make the students want to revise their own display-message to bring it more into line with institutional norms.

Variation

Could your language learners have a web site on the institution's web page? It would be good for the students' morale to be publishing in this format, and they might even receive messages as a result. Being a web site, it would need to be updated regularly, which would ensure on-going work.

6.14   In-writing instruction   Level 6↑

   Time   Not less than 30 minutes

   Computing function   E-mail

   Process stage   Drafting

Preparation

This activity can only work as a computer-based writing exercise if internal-mails are delivered without delay on your network. Check with your IT services department to make sure that your students will get any messages you send without a significant delay.

Procedure

1 Divide the class into pairs or groups of three if you have enough computers to allow this. Assign a writing topic – this can be a story, letter or informative piece of writing.

2 Ask the students to write their composition as an e-mail message which they are going to send to you when it's completed. Explain that you are going to send them an e-mail message every so often which will contain an instruction which they should obey in their writing. If their e-mail system doesn't automatically tell them that they have new messages, tell them to check for new messages every three minutes.

3 Once the students have begun writing, send the first message. Keep sending messages at random intervals thereafter. Your messages can be of any kind, including:
   – introduce a new character into your story in the next sentence
   – make the last sentence you have written negative
   – use an adjective in the next sentence you write
   – use parentheses in the next sentence you write
   – use quotation marks in the next sentence
   – copy and amend the last sentence your neighbour wrote as the next sentence in your own writing.

4 Allow time to discuss the effect of your instructions. Listen carefully to the discussion as you can often learn a lot about the kind of instructions which help writers and the kind that stretch them.

Follow-up

A hard but interesting homework task is to ask the students to rewrite their work in the form they think it would have taken if they hadn't received your instructions.

Variation

Allow a group to invent the instructions that will interrupt their colleagues' work.

Comment

This idea is possible without computers – it's worth thinking about how you give the in-writing instructions: verbally, written on the board, a written instruction passed from writer to writer, etc.

6.15 Discussing language problems

Level 6↑

Time Mostly out-of-class activity; ten minutes in class

Computing function E-mail

Process stage Evaluating

Rationale

Often students have questions about language that other students can throw light on. In this ongoing activity, the students are encouraged to use each other as sources of information. You can also join in if you have something important to say or if you want the discussion to take a particular direction.

Procedure

Explain that each member of the class should use their e-mail to send messages to classmates about anything interesting they come across that is relevant to their language learning. Their messages can be informative or can ask for help or information. If you want to give an example, you can use this message in which Sara asks about Christmas cards:

> While I am writing the X'mas cards (I will give them to you before holiday), I noticed 1 thing. Sometimes the card says 'joyful X'mas' but sometimes it says 'joyous X'mas'. I want to ask in what ways do the two words 'joyful' & 'joyous' differ? I hope I will hear from you very soon.
>
> © Cambridge University Press 1998

It's also a good thing to make it clear that you will be monitoring students' messages and will expect everyone to play an active role in the e-mail discussion. Make sure that you join in the discussion yourself and from time to time take up interesting points in class.

Variation

You can use the same device for getting students to seek each other's advice on their work. It works well if you ask the students to ask the person whose name comes after theirs in the alphabet to have a look at a paragraph of their writing and give feedback on it by e-mail. Make sure that all these messages are copied to you – even if you don't have time to monitor them all as carefully as you would want, it still gives the students the impression that they are getting individual attention and ensures that they take helping each other seriously.

Comment

This is a form of learning in which the students get to introduce the topics that they are interested in. The subject matter is of their own devising, but you will quickly be able to influence the way they write in this medium. For example, if you send a message to the class and sign off 'Best!', you can be sure that your students will start to imitate this form of sign-off and quickly devise their own variations on it. Or if you use a standardised signature, your students will soon teach themselves how to write their own signature files.

6.16 Keeping electronic journals   Level 7↑

Time   Ongoing work

Computing function   E-mail

Process stages   Targeting; organising; drafting; evaluating

Rationale

The aim of this activity is to have students keep their journals in computer files as well as in hard copy. This means that they can send you entries as they write them. They can also react to any comments you make within the writing process rather than take them as a summative comment, as would be the case with traditional hard-copy journals.

Preparation

This activity will work best with classes that are used to keeping language journals in hard-copy form. So if your students have no experience of keeping journals, try a term in which you ask them to record anything interesting they notice in the written or spoken English around them, any strategies they have developed to assist their language learning, any independent learning they do, any English films they see or books they read, anything interesting from English language television around them, any comments they want to make about their status as

English speakers in relation to their own families and friends, etc. Make sure that you read the journals every three weeks or so. (It's a good idea to read one-third of them each week.) Try not to correct language errors unless specifically asked to – instead respond to the content with comments that will encourage students' interest and boost their confidence. Where you are genuinely interested in something, say so. It's particularly important that your tone is non-judgemental.

Procedure

Once your students are familiar with the idea of keeping a personal language journal, ask them to try keeping it as a computer file for a term. Each time they write an entry, they should copy it to you. If they don't receive a reply in three days, they should print it out and add it to their hard-copy journal file. But if you do reply, they can also print your reply and any reaction to it that they have. Usually you will be able to send them a simple acknowledgement even when you haven't time to say much more.

Follow-up

If you want to give a grade for their journals, it's a good idea to ask your students to submit a profile of their work rather than their whole journal – for example, three entries they were pleased with, one where they were disappointed, one where your comment helped them a lot, etc. Explain that the profile grade doesn't mean you haven't read all their work and aren't taking it all into account – in fact, as they know, you have read everything and have been keeping an informal record of the quality of their work. Also insist that they write a short accompanying page explaining why they have chosen the items that they are submitting rather than some others.

Comment

All too often teachers' comments are summative. Keeping an electronic journal and using e-mail as a way of submitting work means that from time to time you will be able to make comments which change the writing that the students actually commit themselves to. Moreover, your students have a strong sense of their close relationship with you even if you are only able to offer comments on every second or third piece of work they share with you. They also often feel that e-mail is a safer medium and allows them to share their problems without embarrassment.

7   Outcomes

The activities in this section all lead to extended, formal outcomes, such as essays or reports. They are grouped according to the kind of writing to which they lead: stories (1–5), letters (6–8), instructions (9–11), business writing (12–14) and academic writing (15–17). Within each category, the activities are arranged in order from simplest to most challenging.

7.1   Writing an account   Level 5↑

Time   50 minutes

Materials   An item from the *News in Brief* column in the newspaper

Process stages   Organising; drafting

Rationale

In this activity, the students describe a series of events leading up to a newsworthy situation. The chronological mode practised here helps to break writing down into a set of separate sentences.

Preparation

Make an OHT of a news item taken from the *News in Brief* column in the newspaper. Choose an item where it's relatively easy to imagine a sequence of events leading up to the situation described in the news item. You may like to use one of the items on the opposite page.

Procedure

1 Display the prepared OHT. Ask your students to close their eyes and imagine the events that led up to the event reported in the newspaper item. The events might have taken place over a few minutes or hours

or over several days or weeks. You may want to suggest that 5–6 events is about the right number.

2 Each student should decide on the date and time of each of these events and note them down in the order in which they occurred.

3 Ask the students to write an account of these events starting at the beginning and working forwards through time.

4 Encourage the students to get together with their neighbours to compare their chronologies.

- A woman who had her car towed away when she parked illegally on a bridge yesterday got home and found she had won a new car in a competition organised by the Council who had towed her car away.
- A man who gave up his job to look after his sick mother must sell his home to pay for her care, a judge ruled yesterday.
- A man who was bitten by a dog and then bit it in return has been ordered to pay the dog's owner £100 compensation.
- When a bank clerk refused to accept a present of a box of chocolates from an elderly customer, she moved her account to another bank.
- A woman sentenced to a month's imprisonment after repeatedly stealing food from a supermarket has gone on hunger strike in prison.
- A couple who got divorced last year remarried yesterday after being matched by a computer dating service.
- A headteacher in north London has introduced a good table manners module into the school curriculum after observing pupils eating their school dinners.

Variations

i Ask the students to try their hand at rewriting the account in the chronological order they think the newspaper reporter would adopt.

ii Ask the students to write a more connected record, perhaps starting with *It began when* … .You may find it helpful to suggest connectives such as *then* and *after that*.

iii Ask the students to work in small groups and write a short connected piece answering the question *Why did this happen?* Completed writing can be passed from one group to another. More advanced groups who can handle suppositional language can be given the title *Why do you think this happened?*

7.2 Stories: reducing stories

Level 5↑

Time 20–45 minutes

Materials A simple story

Process stage Rewriting

Rationale

If your students have too little English to write a full story, give them a full story and ask them to make a summary of it.

Preparation

You will need to find a simple story either from the class reader or from a collection such as *40 short short stories*. You will need enough copies so that there is one for each student.

Procedure

1 The students may work individually or in pairs. Distribute the short stories and explain that they must rewrite them in their own words, but that they are allowed just one sentence for each paragraph of the original. Exclude dialogue from this.
2 Allow time for the results to be read aloud.

Follow-up

You can use these outlines as input with a more advanced class. Ask them to expand the outline.

Variation

You can vary the 'one-sentence-to-a-paragraph' rule. For example, you can allow one sentence of the original to be copied as well as a one-sentence summary of the rest of the paragraph. Or give a word limit.

7.3   Stories: expanding stories   Level 6↑

Time   40 minutes

Materials   A story outline

Process stage   Drafting: from outline to text

Preparation

You need a story outline – either consult John Morgan and Mario Rinvolucri's *Once Upon a Time,* or use either of the outlines provided, or write your own. If you're writing your own, a good technique is to base your outline on a story you've read. The outline on the next page is based on Albert Camus's short story *The Guest.* Make enough copies of your outline so that there is one for each student.

Procedure

1 Divide the class into five groups. (If you have a large class, divide it into two or more sets and each set into five groups.) Distribute the story outlines and allocate one of the five sections to each group. Ask each group to write their part of the story. Set a word limit – we suggest 60–90 words.
2 Allow time for the stories to be read aloud and commented on.

---

1 Every day on the way to work, Brian gets on the train one station before Samantha. She gets off one station before him. They fall in love with each other. They have never spoken.
2 Neither knows for sure that the other person loves them. Their feelings begin to interfere with their work.
3 Just before St Valentine's Day, she decides to buy him a card and hand it over before she gets off the train on St Valentine's Day. She buys the card.
4 On the train on St Valentine's Day, she is ready to hand it over just before she gets off the train.
5 Just before she is about to hand the card over, he gives her a card. She is too surprised to give him the one she had bought him. She opens the card he gave her after she gets off the train. He has chosen the same card for her as she had chosen for him!

© Cambridge University Press 1998

---

1 A policeman brings a prisoner to a school during the school holidays when only the teacher is there. He tells the teacher to take the prisoner to the magistrate in the next town the following day.
2 The teacher treats the prisoner kindly, makes him a meal and gives him a bed for the night.
3 The next morning, the teacher makes the prisoner breakfast, talks to him about the crime he has committed, and sets off with him towards the town.
4 They stop at the top of a hill. The teacher gives the prisoner money and food, and points out the town where the magistrate is waiting and a village where the prisoner will find his friends.
5 The teacher leaves the prisoner. Later, he looks back and sees ...

© Cambridge University Press 1998

Follow-up

Now that you have a story in five sections, you can work on it in class with the purpose of producing a more polished final version.

7.4 Bilingual stories 1 Level 5↑

Time 40 minutes

Materials A very simple story (see *Preparation*)

Process stage Drafting: expanding an outline

Preparation

Make a copy of a very simple story for each student. The St Valentine's Day story in **6.6 Expressing a viewpoint** works well.

Procedure

1 The students can work individually or in pairs. Distribute copies of the story to the students and ask them to rewrite it so that the thoughts of one of the characters are written into the story in their mother tongue. It's a good idea to give an example of what you're looking for. You can start the activity as a whole-class activity and

then get the students to continue it individually or in pairs. For **6.6** you might start in the following way (we use italics where your students would use their mother tongue):

> Two people who travel to work on the same train fall in love with each other. *I fell in love with him the first time I saw him.* They have never spoken. *But I never dared to speak to him – the train was always so crowded.* Neither knows … .

2 As you will get a range of different stories with the same outline, they are very interesting to hear read aloud or to use in a wall display.

Variations

Bilingual stories can take many forms:

i   The narrative can be written in English and the dialogue can be written in the mother tongue.
ii   There can be two narrators, an English-speaking one and a mother-tongue one.
iii The text can consist of a series of switches from one language to another at points decided by the writer.
iv   The story can consist of third-person narrative in English and first-person narrative in the mother tongue.
v   The reader can be directly addressed in English and the story can be told in the mother tongue.
vi   Or more simply, the students write the story in English using mother-tongue words and phrases when they are stuck.

7.5   **Bilingual stories 2**   Level 7↑

Time   50 minutes

Process stages   Planning; drafting

Rationale

Using the first language from time to time gives writers the confidence to say exactly what they want to and loosens them up to write more freely in the second language as well. At a higher level, writers don't need this prop, but sometimes still enjoy the special effects it creates.

Procedure

1 Students work in pairs and together plan the story they will write. You may, if you wish, suggest a topic, such as someone's search for a lost pet or for a colleague who suddenly goes absent at work. Explain that the story must contain dialogue and that the students must agree what happens before anything can be written down.

2 Ask the students to write their stories, but without conferring. One student writes the story with all the dialogue in the first language and the narrative in English, while the other writes the dialogue in English and the rest in the mother tongue.

3 When they have finished, ask the students to compare their stories. Encourage class discussion of places where the mother tongue and English language versions differed markedly. They should also discuss which version was easier to write and why.

Variation

Vary the storyline slightly so that it is an English person who is searching for a pet (or missing colleague) in the students' country. The questions the searcher asks are in English but the replies are in the students' first language. Or reverse the roles so that the story takes place in an English-speaking country. The questions are in the students' mother tongue and the answers are in English.

Comment

Bilingual stories often have something about them that monolingual stories do not have. This means that the students sense they have created something genuinely original even when they have limited English.

7.6 Letters expressing opinions

Level 7↑

Time   50 minutes

Process stages   Planning; drafting

Rationale

In many countries, there is a television programme featuring viewers' letters. In Britain, this programme is called *Viewpoint* and is made up of lots of short letters from viewers about television programmes. As television viewers, your students already have knowledge and opinions about the programmes they watch which can be tapped as a basis for writing a letter.

Procedure

1 Discuss the kinds of letters viewers write to *Viewpoint*. If there isn't a *Viewpoint* programme in your country, discuss the kinds of letters viewers might want to write about the programmes they see. In classes where the students share a common first language, this discussion works well if they use the mother tongue and you use English. Also decide on the broadcaster they would choose as an ideal presenter. The presenter needs to be able to introduce each letter in a few words, for example, *'Jane Wellings was also disappointed with the Saturday night schedule'* or *'Many viewers were very enthusiastic about "The Making of a Maestro". John Legg writes ...'*.
2 Ask each student to decide which programme they would like to write a letter about. If two students have similar views on the same programme, allow them to work together. Allow 20 minutes for writing the letter which should be addressed to the presenter of the local *Viewpoint* programme (if it exists) or to the presenter chosen in Step 1.
3 Ask the students to make a wall display of the letters.

Follow-ups

If you have a camcorder, you can have some of the letters read aloud and recorded as a *Viewpoint* programme. Good letters can also be rewritten in the mother tongue and sent to the television company.

Variation

In many countries there are also consumer affairs programmes which investigate viewers' complaints about goods and services. Get the students to discuss unfortunate experiences with goods or services and write letters of complaint.

7.7 Letters for others

Level 7↑

Time Around 45 minutes

Process stage Planning and drafting

Rationale

We are all likely on occasions to be asked to write something on behalf of someone else. In this activity, your students have a chance to do this in English. Note that this activity works best with adults.

Procedure

1 Ask your students to make a list of the last three extended pieces of writing they either did for someone else or helped someone else to do. They might have written a letter for a member of their family to the bank, for example, or helped a friend to write a letter of application for a job, or written a letter to the school on behalf of their children, or written a memo at work for their boss. These letters will probably have been written in their first language, although it's just possible that some might have been written in English. If any student can't think of anything they helped someone else write, ask them to imagine three occasions on which they might be asked to write something for someone else.

2 Allow a few minutes for each student to find one or two other students who have recently done one of the kinds of writing for someone else that they have. They should settle down as a pair or group of three and do a similar piece of writing in English.

Follow-up

There is likely to be quite a range of different types of writing resulting from this activity – so you can ask one or two groups to talk about their work.

Variation

A possible variation for children is to ask them to write out the instructions that they want their parents to follow in writing a letter on their behalf to the school or to a company they want to inquire about buying something from.

7.8   Letters to superiors   Level 8↑

Time   40 minutes

Process stages   Planning; organising; drafting

Rationale

This letter could well serve as a model for a real-world piece of functional writing that your students will write at work, and which, if the outcome is successful, can only have a beneficial effect on their English.

Procedure

1 Get your class to brainstorm all the reasons why they need more language training. Write these ideas on the board.
2 Give the students a choice of either working alone, in pairs or in small groups. Each student/group then writes a letter or memo to their boss or headteacher or head of department explaining their need for language training and requesting company or school or university department support for it. This support could include time off work, in-house training, etc. (companies), and more time and better facilities, equipment and materials, etc. (schools). It's a good idea to stress that each group should think carefully about the ordering of the contents of the letter. Go around giving assistance with this where appropriate.

Variation

If you work in a school, ask your students to work in small groups brainstorming all the needs they might have for English when they start work. They then write a letter to you explaining their future needs and suggesting ways of making the language classes as relevant as possible. This is a useful step on the road to a negotiated syllabus.

7.9 Writing directions Level 6↑

Time At least 75 minutes (which can be spread over more than one lesson)

Process stages Organising; drafting; evaluating; editing

Rationale

The aim of this activity is to have the class produce a useful set of written directions for finding their (language) school for visitors coming from overseas, from somewhere else in the same country, or on foot.

Preparation

Decide on a number of different starting points from which visitors to your school might set out. Then decide on the appropriate means of transport from each starting point. For example, visitors might come by plane and bus/train, by train, by car from one of several directions, on foot from the station, etc.

Procedure

1 Divide the class into as many equal-sized groups as you have routes to write directions for. Allow the groups sufficient time to draft the written directions they would send to a visitor coming by the route allocated. Each group should agree their version of the directions they are responsible for writing, and each member of the group must make a copy of them.
2 Ask the students to regroup in such a way as to ensure that the new groups contain just one person from each of the original groups. So if you had five original groups, there will be five students in each new group. The new groups should work through all the directions that each student has brought and make any necessary improvements to them.
3 When the groups have made their improvements, the students should return to their original groups and produce a final version of their directions.

Follow-up

If possible, have the students make a neat word-processed version of these instructions to send to the school Principal as a possible set of directions to supply to visitors.

Variations

i   You can use the same idea for writing directions for visitors to the students' workplaces or homes.

ii You can also have the students compile a directory of useful local information, including places to visit/things to see, sports facilities, restaurants, entertainment, night-life, public transport, shopping, doing what the locals do, free or low-cost activities, etc. Small groups of students can be assigned particular topic areas.

7.10 Instructions – writing about interests   Level 6↑

Time   30–40 minutes

Process stages   Planning; organising; drafting

Procedure

1 Explain that the students will write about something that they are experts in and enthusiastic about. It could be a hobby such as fishing or a leisure activity such as swimming or going to the disco. They may write alone or with a partner, but if they work with a partner, both students must be genuinely enthusiastic about the topic they write about. Explain that the writing will follow the format of recipes, with a list of things needed and a description of what to do with them. So for a disco, *What you need* would include a group of friends, money, a Friday night, the right clothes, etc. Allow 30 minutes for writing. Encourage the use of dictionaries and go around offering help where necessary.

2 Display the results on the wall.

Variation

The focus of this activity is on the topic. If you want the students to focus on readership, ask them to write in such a way as to encourage the reader to try the interest described for themselves.

Comment

Notice that this differs from the usual interest essay in which the writers simply explain why they are interested in a hobby or other activity. The recipe format enables readers to visualise the activity and possibly even carry it out themselves.

7.11 Guides

Level 8↑

Time 45 minutes

Materials Copies or photocopies of part of a printed guide in the students' first language to the city or a monument in the city where they live

Process stage Drafting

Rationale

One of the real-world things students of English sometimes have to do is to translate from their first language into English for the sake of English-speaking visitors. This exercise gives practice in that activity.

Procedure

1 Divide the class into pairs. Distribute the copies of the guide. If the guide is lengthy, you can divide it into sections of no more than 200 words for distribution to different pairs.
2 Ask the students in their pairs to read through their section. Each pair may ask three questions about difficult vocabulary before getting down to translating their passage.
3 When the students have finished, they should join another pair translating the same passage and compare results. They should try to agree on a best translation.
4 If there is an English version already in existence, you can compare it with the students' work and decide on the strengths and weaknesses of each translation.

Variations

i   You can encourage free rather than exact translations if you wish.
ii If your students are adults and attached to a firm, translating some of their material is another possibility.
iii The instructions for such things as electrical goods are a rich field for such translation, particularly if there is an English version available which you can use as a standard of comparison at Step 4.

7.12   Report writing   Level 7↑

Time   90 minutes (can be spread over two lessons)
Process stages   Planning; organising; drafting

Procedure

1 Divide the class into groups of three. Ask the groups to discuss their engagement with English in the past month. They may find themselves discussing English lessons, other lessons where English is used, homework, out-of-class activities such as learning vocabulary lists, conversing in English, hearing English spoken, watching English language television, reading newspapers and magazines, etc. Each student should make brief notes as they talk.

2 The class as a whole discuss what names to give each category of English experience. It's possible that the discussion will lead to considering major divisions such as formal/informal use or active/passive experience. Encourage the students to think about the secondary divisions within these broad categories. This will provide headings and sub-headings and also essential vocabulary for the task which follows. So for example there might be two main headings *In class* and *Out of class*, with sub-headings such as *listening*, *grammar* and *measuring progress* under *In class*, and *at work*, *at home* and *leisure use* under *Out of class*.

3 Explain that each group will write a short report on their engagement with English. They should decide who they are writing their report for: perhaps a similar institution where staff and students are keen to compare language learning experiences. They should think about how to begin their report: reports very often start by stating their purpose and the data-base they will describe. Each group will need to decide on the title of the report as well as on the headings and contents of the sections.

4 As you sense that most groups are close to completing their reports, suggest that the summary of their reports might include a comment on the effectiveness of their language learning.

Variations

i   The report can be preceded by a daily diary of the student's engagement with English.

ii   A survey of the language-learning activities of the class as a whole is a more complex data-base, but makes a more satisfying basis for a report.

iii A subsequent evaluative essay could have as its title: *How effective have your language-learning activities over the past month been?* The difference between the diary, the report, and the essay are worth discussing.

iv Alternatively, the class can be divided into three groups – one working on a diary, one on a report, and one on an essay.

v You may prefer a different topic that the class has personal knowledge of, such as television watching habits.

7.13 Memos   Level 7↑

Time 30 minutes (first writing task), plus 20 minutes (Steps 3 and 4)

Materials If available, memo forms for each student

Process stages Targeting; drafting; editing

Level Adults

Rationale

Memos are a particularly interesting form of writing because they are semi-formal, supposed to have only a single topic, relate to a previous situation and look ahead to an outcome. This means that for adults used to working in organisations where memos are used, this form of writing is already well understood. The students therefore bring considerable knowledge of the genre to the classroom task.

Procedure

1 Discuss the kinds of memo your students receive at work and the typical properties of a written memo.

2 If you have headed memo forms, distribute these. Alternatively, you can copy the form below.

MEMORANDUM	
From	To ....
cc	Date ....
Subject	

© Cambridge University Press 1998

3 Ask the students to draft the memo they would least like to receive at work. Make sure they indicate who the memo is from.
4 Pair the students and ask each to explain to their partner why the memo they have written is so unwelcome.
5 Each student then writes a reply to the memo their partner has written.

Variations

We are grateful to an anonymous reader of an earlier draft of this book for suggesting that this idea could be extended to include the menu you would least like to be offered at a dinner party or the letter you would least like to receive from your boyfriend or girlfriend as well as the memo, menu or letter you would most like to receive. Other categories for the most desirable/least desirable treatment include written telephone messages, written invitations, letters from the bank, school reports – the list is endless.

Follow-up

You can also set the writing as a homework task and ask for the memos to be word-processed.

7.14   Minutes   Level 8↑

> **Time**   40 minutes
>
> **Process stages**   Targeting; drafting; editing; evaluating

Rationale

In the real world outside the classroom, most institutions are run by committees at which minutes are taken. Yet we rarely teach this skill as an outcome in either the first- or second-language class. By using the activities of the class itself as the subject of the minute-taking, students are taking a careful look at what is going on and making a written record of it.

Procedure

1 Divide the class into two halves, either front/back or left-hand side/right-hand side. Explain that you are going to teach one group and that the other group are to act as secretaries taking minutes.

2 Accept suggestions for the format of the start of the minutes. Work towards agreeing something like:

> Minutes of lesson taught to ‹name of class›
> ‹date›
> ‹list of those absent›

3 Teach half the class for up to ten minutes while the secretaries keep a record of the key points of the lesson.
4 When you have finished teaching, pair each secretary with someone from the other group, who has to check that it is a correct record and should suggest any changes that are needed. Once the record is agreed and a final copy has been made, it can be brought to you to be signed.
5 Discuss the importance of recording only the main points of the lesson and not all the minor details.
6 Display the minutes on the wall for interest and comparison.

Follow-ups

1 The first time you try this activity, the minutes are unlikely to read very authentically. If you have time, it's a good idea to produce your own set to distribute.
2 If your students attend meetings outside class, they can be asked to take minutes as a homework task.

Comment

Though this is classroom based, it reflects a real-world activity. It also provides a rare opportunity for the students to observe and reflect on what is going on in the classroom.

7.15 Assessed essays – examination preparation

Level 8↑

Time   Lesson 1 – 40 minutes; Lesson 2 or homework – 40 minutes

Materials   Copy of FCE exam paper or comparable local exam

Process stages   Planning; organising; drafting

Rationale

Your students may well one day be preparing for an external examination such as Cambridge First Certificate or a local equivalent. Preparing one of the essay questions can be practised from intermediate level onwards. One of the questions in FCE and most comparable exams requires candidates to choose a topic based on one of the essay types listed below.

1   a short story
2   a description of a person, place or topic
3   a 'For and against' essay
4   a formal or informal letter
5   a speech

45 minutes are allotted for the essay and the word limit is 120–180 words.

Procedure: Lesson 1

1   Ask the students to look at the copy of the exam paper they will one day be taking. Discuss the length, timing and selection of the essay question. Explain that the class will be practising the 'For and against' essay and will plan an essay on the title *'The Internet does more harm than good.' Do you agree?*
2   Divide the class into two groups – perhaps according to birthday, i.e. January–June and July–December. Invite the first group to give as many reasons in favour of the Internet as they can, recording the results of their brainstorming on the board or OHP, and then do the same for the second group, who will give reasons against. Group together points and highlight them in preparation for writing an essay on the theme.

3 Discuss possible essay plans. For instance, someone who foresaw more opportunities than dangers in the use of the Internet might end up with a plan such as:
   – Introduction
   – Minor points against
   – Points for
   – Conclusion (i.e. one's own opinion)
4 It may be worth brainstorming language to introduce the second paragraph, for example, *Opponents of the Internet make a few minor points such as ...* or *Before coming to the important points in favour of the Internet ...* , and for the third paragraph *However, there is much to be said in favour of the Internet ...* or *The arguments in favour of the Internet are much stronger.*
5 Now that you have practised drawing up an essay plan as a whole class, ask the students to work in pairs and give them another 'For and against' title. They should go through the brainstorming and planning stages.

Lesson 2

One member of each pair writes the 'for' essay and the other writes the 'against' essay. This can be done in class under strict exam conditions, or it can be a homework task. Depending on the experience of your students, you may need to draw their attention to the advantages of drafting a rough version first and working to improve this draft before carefully copying out a final version.

7.16   Making lecture notes   Level 8↑

> **Time**   45 minutes
>
> **Materials**   Highlighters if available
>
> **Process stages**   Drafting; editing

Preparation

Prepare a short lecture of 15 minutes on a topic of general interest to your class. If you are going to use the *Variation*, you will need to type the lecture and make photocopies.

Procedure

1 Explain that you will give a 15-minute lecture while the students take notes. The lecture can be in the form of a very simple talk to suit the capabilities of your particular students.
2 Ask the students to form pairs and swap their notes. Each student should underline or highlight key items.
3 Partners should then discuss the two versions.
4 The underlined/highlighted notes can be written out neatly as a homework task. The two versions make a good wall display.

Follow-up

Ask the students to write a short essay of their own based on the key notes.

Variation

Half the class are given copies of the lecture after the note-taking stage and highlight the key points on the lecture text itself, while the rest carry out Step 2 above. Pair up students from each group to compare results.

Acknowledgement

This activity was thought out in this form by Emily Monastiriotis, Kirsty Arnell and Lisa Huddart.

7.17   Tabulating and explaining   Level 8↑

Time   50 minutes

Process stages   Organising; drafting

Rationale

Much written material contains tables which incorporate information that can be seen at a glance. The making of such a table is a specialised written outcome and explaining it and pointing out its significance is another. It is not always easy to find suitable tables to write about, so we suggest a simple game-like activity to provide tabulated data for your students to write about.

Procedure

1 Write a short sentence on the board or OHP with only the first letter
of each word given and spaces to indicate the number of letters in the
word. So if your sentence was *Learning to write seems easier in this
class*, you would write on the board:

1 L _ _ _ _ _ _ _
2 t _
3 w _ _ _ _
4 s _ _ _ _
5 e _ _ _ _ _
6 i _
7 t _ _ _
8 c _ _ _ _

Ask your students to guess each of the words one-by-one starting
with the first word, and then going on to the second word, and then
on through the sentence. Allow a maximum of ten guesses for each
word before you give the answer. Appoint a scorer and a timekeeper.
The scorer records the number of tries it takes to guess each word
and the timekeeper records the number of seconds it takes.

2 When the sentence is complete, make a simple table showing the
number of guesses and the time each took:

Word	Number of guesses	Time in seconds
Learning		
to		
write		
seems		
easier		
in		
this		
class		

3 Divide the class into pairs and allow 5–10 minutes to discuss the
table, referring to such things as which was the easiest word to guess,
which the hardest, which took the shortest and which the longest
time. More advanced students can speculate as to why some words
took longer.

4 Allow 20 minutes for writing-up time: each pair should produce an
account of the information shown in the table.

Variation

You can repeat this activity with two different sentences leading to two tables. The students can be encouraged to write about the differences between the tables and to speculate on the reasons for these differences.

Comment

Adjust the sentence to the level of interest and language ability of your students. This kind of activity has two useful outcomes – the table and the comment on it.

8 Assessment

The activities in this section are designed to help you to shift some of the responsibility for assessing writing to the students you teach. Activities 1–3 give the students practice in designing assessment measures themselves. In Activities 4 and 5, they act as assessors of writing done outside the classroom by others. The rest of the activities, 6–17, are ordered so that those involving self-assessment are placed earlier and those involving assessment by others are placed later. Activities 13 and 14 call for unconventional forms of assessment which test the communicative effectiveness of the writing.

8.1 Making a pre-writing checklist   Level 6↑

Time   15 minutes

Process stages   Planning and evaluating; measuring outcome against plan

Rationale

The purpose of this activity is to make a checklist which the students complete as a pre-writing activity so that they can refer to it once their writing is completed.

Procedure

1 Ask the students to think about all the questions that they should ask themselves before they start to write. Where necessary, hint at areas they might suggest. Write their questions up on the board. These should include at least:
   - What do I need to find out that I don't know before I start to write? Where will I get this information?
   - Who am I writing for? What impression do I want to make on my reader(s)?
   - What are the main points I want to make?

– How should I organise my material?

– What conclusion do I want to reach?

2 Once you have agreed the items, decide on the order they should be listed in. (The order above seems logical.) Once you have agreed on the order, ask the students to copy the checklist.

3 Discuss to what extent the students already ask themselves these questions before they begin to write. Discuss the extent to which they think about their answers to these pre-writing questions while they are writing.

Follow-up

Now that you have made a checklist, you should obviously use it when your students have writing tasks which will result in outcomes. It's a good idea to type it up with appropriate spaces left for answers and then make a copy for each student. Allow 15 minutes for them to complete it before they begin to write, and a further few minutes to explain their decisions to a classmate. When the writing is complete, ask the students to return to the completed checklist and note any areas in which their writing turned out differently from the way they had expected.

Comment

As more and more of our writing is word-processed, it is all the time becoming easier for us to produce and edit drafts. Therefore checking that we have in fact done what we intended to do becomes a more realistic task since we can easily make any changes that we feel necessary.

8.2 Inventing descriptors   Level 10↑

Time Lesson 1 – 30 minutes; Lesson 2 – 20 minutes

Process stage Evaluation: defining criteria

'Descriptors' are descriptions of what is achieved at a particular level and are used as a measure or indication of attainment. The International English Language Testing Service (IELTS) has nine descriptors, each corresponding to a 'band' in a spectrum which goes from no significant knowledge of English to near native-speaker ability.

Rationale

Often your students will have quite a sophisticated idea of the criteria for good writing. In this activity you draw on their expertise and help them to frame their ideas as descriptors so that they can then apply them to their own work. In this way, they have a role in defining the standards by which they are to be judged.

Procedure: Lesson 1

1 Explain that you want to construct four descriptions of writing, one for good writing, one for above-average writing, one for below-average writing and one for poor writing. Explain that these descriptions should cover as many aspects of writing as possible. Begin by asking for suggestions as to the different elements involved in writing and list them on the board.

2 Once you have a reasonable list, which should include at least organisation of material, quality of expression, relevance to topic, readership awareness, appearance on the page and accuracy, ask your students either in whole-class mode or working in groups to suggest ways of describing these aspects at each of the four levels of writing. Write suggestions on the board.

3 Explain that you will take note of the students' suggestions and come to the next class with your own descriptions of good writing, above-average writing, below-average writing and poor writing which will be based on the students' suggestions. You may like to use the descriptors on the opposite page as a basis for your own.

Lesson 2

1 Either hand out copies of your descriptors or write them up on the board. Ask for comments and suggestions which could improve them. When you are willing to accept a suggestion, amend the descriptor on the board or, if the students have copies, ask them to amend these.

2 Once the descriptors are agreed, ask the students to spend 15–20 minutes checking through their previous writing in order to decide on their band. They should indicate which band they think their writing falls into in their exercise books so that you can comment on it when you next take their books in.

– Good writing is organised so that the developing argument is clear to the reader throughout. Good writing is relevant to the topic at every stage, shows awareness of target readership and takes account of the likely attitude of the reader to the content of the writing. Good writing is fluent, easy to read and well presented on the page.

– Above-average writing is well-organised, relevant to the topic, shows awareness of readership, is written in fluent, accurate English, and is well presented on the page.

– Below-average writing is organised only to some degree, is not always relevant to the topic, appears to have a target reader in mind from time to time, and is written in English which is intelligible but not always accurate. The presentation on the page could be improved.

– Poor writing shows little organisation or awareness of the target reader. It is frequently difficult to determine the topic or the stage of its development. In places the English is unintelligible and generally the style makes comprehension hard work for the reader. The presentation is poor.

© Cambridge University Press 1998

Variation

Obviously the level of delicacy of the descriptors will depend upon the age and ability level of your students and the kind of writing they do. We use terms like *good*, *average* and *poor* in the description above. You can obviously substitute terms like *effective* if you have intermediate students.

Comment

One obvious value of this approach is that it enables the students to see where they stand in relation to expected norms. They will also probably feel that in some respects they fall into one band, in other respects into another – this then gives them an idea of which aspect of their writing they need to concentrate on improving. You can also engineer the content of the descriptors in such a way as to indicate what you consider important in judging writing at your students' present level.

8.3   Writing a task instruction 1   Level 5↑

Time   30 minutes

Process stage   Planning: preparing to write

Rationale

Most teachers of writing agree that it isn't fair to assess students' writing unless the task has been fully defined so that all the students have an equal chance of completing it in the designated way. This activity invites the students to play a part in defining the way writing is tested and scored, in this case by involving them in the definition of the task prior to assessing the extent to which they have successfully fulfilled it.

Preparation

Prepare one topic to write about for every four students in your class. These topics should be described as very general instructions. Good examples include *Write a letter, Give advice on buying a radio, Recommend a holiday, Describe the house you hope to buy, Describe the town you live in.*

Procedure

1 Discuss the importance of knowing exactly what you are to write about and who you are to write it for. Explain that when you ask your students to write, you usually try to give them sufficient information for them to know exactly what you are expecting them to do. For example, you would not ask a class just to write about buying a car. Instead you would specify the purposes for which the car was required, the local conditions in which it was to be used, the degree of experience and broad preferences of the driver/s, etc., and then ask the class to make some suggestions that would be likely to meet the driver's needs.

2 Ask the students to work in groups of four. Give each group one of your general topics. Ask them to provide a detailed brief for a task relating to the topic in the form of an instruction that a teacher might use.

Variations

i Ask each student to add one specifying element to the writing task before passing it on to their neighbour, who then adds a further specifying element. This is a very interesting activity because each specifying element usually requires a rewrite of the whole task.

ii Another possibility is to ask the students to think about a general task in their workplace, such as how would you entertain a visitor to your company from an English-speaking country. The students then have to make this a much more exactly specified task.

8.4   Writing a task instruction 2   Level 8↑

Time   20–25 minutes

Materials   Texts (see *Preparation*)

Process stage   Evaluation

Rationale

This activity gives practice in evaluating writing as a successful task-completion exercise.

Preparation

You need to have a text, or, if you want variety, three or four different texts. Often a coursebook text will work well or, if you're working with professional adults, an authentic text from their workplace. Letters, public notices and descriptions of places or events are all good. If the text is not in the coursebook, make a copy for each student. You will find a letter that works well on the next page.

Procedure

1 The students can work individually or in pairs. Distribute the text/s and ask the students to read it/them carefully. Clarify any vocabulary problems. Ask the students to write a description of the writing task as a set of instructions which the writer would have needed to follow to produce the text which they are reading.

2 Compare results and, optionally, work towards a prototype, or best example.

PERSONAL

Dear Mr Brookes,

<u>YOU</u> ARE A WINNER!

To get the Money your Lucky Number 6308146 has DEFINITELY won – simply fill in and return the 'Cash Claim' attached to the 'OFFICIAL WINNER'S NOTIFICATION' included with this letter.

What has Lucky Number 6308146 won for you, Mr Brookes?

It can be the £30,000.00 TOP CASH AWARD! Or maybe one of TEN £500.00 cash WINS or FIVE £1,000.00 Money Awards! Maybe a SURPRISE Runner-Up MONEY WIN? Or even the DOUBLE TOP AWARD of £60,000.00!!

Just sign the 'Cash Claim' and return it NOW! Don't let the good fortune of <u>your</u> WIN and what can be <u>your</u> surprisingly Lucky Number go to someone else!

Yours sincerely,

Steve Pound

Steve Pound
Director

P.S. Claim your confirmed Cash Win – post your 'Cash Claim' today!

Variation

Much more ambitiously, you can ask the students to set themselves individual writing tasks for homework. In class, they exchange the outcomes with partners and then each writes what they take the task description to have been. If you try this, it's best to do the version described above first.

8.5 Selecting the best letter   Level 4↑

Time   Steps 1–4 – 30 minutes; Step 5 – 20 minutes

Materials   Letters to newspapers

Process stage   Evaluating

Rationale

By focusing on what the letters editors of popular newspapers look for in selecting the kind of letter they want to print, this activity helps students to understand that very particular kinds of evaluation will be applied to this kind of writing.

Preparation

Choose 5–6 simple letters to popular newspapers and make a copy for each student. Try to choose the letters so that one is the 'letter of the week' or wins a money prize, and the remainder are more ordinary – but don't reveal which is which on your copy. If you have an OHP, make an OHT of one of the ordinary ones. Examples are provided on the next page.

Procedure

1 Divide the class into pairs and display the OHT. If you don't have an OHP, write the letter up on the board. Ask the students to consider a) what made the editor decide to publish this letter, and b) what editors of popular newspapers might be looking for as they read the letters in their postbags.
2 Return to whole-class mode and ask for criteria. As ideas are suggested, write them on the board. Expectable content criteria

I THOUGHT I'd seen every misdemeanour motorists get up to while driving, such as fiddling with radios, pacifying pets and using mobile phones.

The other day I stopped at traffic lights and glanced at the car next to me. I was amazed to see a young woman in the backseat cutting the hair of the driver in front of her.

– R. Smith, Exeter,
Devon

I WAS shocked when I visited my elderly aunt one day and found her coming down a ladder after painting her upstairs windows. I told her she was very foolish to do something so dangerous at her age. 'It's all right,' she replied. 'I put my reading-glasses on for a job like this so the ground doesn't look so far down.'

– Mrs. J. Snow, Barnsley,
W. Yorkshire

AFTER I started a new job, a woman there was introduced as Mickey. 'That's an unusual name for a woman,' I said. 'How did you come by it?'

I wished I hadn't asked. She said: 'It's my nick-name because I look like Mickey Mouse – I've got stick-out ears and round, beady eyes.' Fortunately she was easy-going and took her nick-name very well.

– Mrs P. Sutherland, Kendal,
Cumbria

EXHAUSTED after helping at a local playgroup, I said to a neighbour: 'I should look on the cheery side, kids brighten up the home.' 'Ours certainly do,' she replied. 'They never switch the lights off when they leave a room.'

– Mrs K. McKay, Bearsden,
Glasgow

I WAS frowning at my grand-daughter because she was making a mess with her food. When she asked if I was cross, I looked at her angelic face and answered: 'Of course not, sweetheart.'

'You might not be, but your eyebrows are,' she said.

– Nancy Turner,
Croydon, London

include brevity, interest value, relation to topical event or previous letter, catching attention at the beginning, providing human interest examples to support the point made, humour, finishing with a strong sentence.

3 When the list is complete, ask the class to decide which are the most important criteria. Number them accordingly. Try to guide the discussion so that the students decide which are most important from the editor's perspective.

4 Distribute the sheet with all the letters on it and ask the students to work in pairs and agree the order in which the letters would appeal to an editor. Ask them to try to identify which is the 'letter of the week'.

5 Each student, having noted the criteria, should write a letter either in class or for homework. When these letters have been written, they may be discussed in pairs. Alternatively, they can be arranged in a wall display according to how successfully they fulfil the criteria.

Comment

As soon as students have sufficient English to discuss criteria, they should be encouraged to do so not only in letter writing, as here, but also in other forms of continuously assessed work and in examinations.

8.6   Drawing up conferencing agendas   Level 4↑

Time   30 minutes, plus five minutes follow-up per student

Process stage   Evaluating

Rationale

The activity is suitable for situations where you are able to give some individual attention to your students – perhaps because you have only a small group, perhaps because you have identified a small group in a larger class for this special attention. We build conferencing into our writing classes, and often hold the conferences outside regular class hours.

Preparation

1 It often helps to draw up an outline agenda sheet before the class. This should contain broad headings like *Questions about accuracy, Questions about vocabulary, Questions about spelling, Questions about content, Any other questions*. If you like, you can make copies of the sheet on the opposite page. Allow enough space between each heading for the students to write in any matters about which they wish to consult you. Encourage them to use formulas like: *Is it better to say x or y?, I don't know how to say x, Should I discuss x or y first?, My dictionary allows 'fulfil' but my spellcheck doesn't – which is right?, I'm not sure how to punctuate the quotation, lines 4–7*.

2 Your students need to have the first draft of a piece of writing they are working on.

Procedure

1 Explain to your students that you intend to offer them the opportunity to hold a short conference with you about the piece of writing which they have just drafted. Explain that they will need to draw up an agenda listing those topics which they would most like to discuss.

2 Ask them to number the lines of their text so that they can refer to questions by line number.

3 Distribute prepared agenda formats and allow up to 15 minutes for the students to draw up their conference agendas.

Follow-up

You will obviously need to make sufficient time to respond to these agendas.

Variations

i   You can limit the areas to form only (the students' questions have to be about accuracy) or to content only.

ii You can put a limit on the number of questions allowed.

iii You can ask students to work in groups of three – the group asks one question relating to the work of each member of the group.

iv Your conference with your students can be in written rather than spoken form. Or by e-mail.

AGENDA SHEET

This is your opportunity to consult me about anything in the piece of writing that you are drafting which you would like advice on or would like to discuss. Before you come and talk to me, please write down your questions in as many of the spaces below as you want to.

Questions about grammar/correctness

Questions about vocabulary

Questions about spelling

Questions about content

Questions about organisation

Any other questions

© Cambridge University Press 1998

8.7 Modifying our purpose

Level 7↑

Time 15 minutes within a writing session

Process stage Evaluating

Rationale

Although we begin to write with a clear purpose in mind, practised writers frequently need to adjust the task as they write. This happens much less frequently in task-driven classroom writing, but is nevertheless an important part of learning to be a good writer.

Preparation

This is an activity which you can introduce while your students are engaged in a writing task which was fully specified for them in advance.

Procedure

1 When your students are half-way through a piece of writing, ask them to stop and look again at the task description in front of them. Ask them to think for two or three minutes about a way in which their writing would be more effective if their task were slightly modified. Perhaps there is some new piece of information which should be included but which was not specified in the original task description. Perhaps if the readership were more fully defined in some respect, their writing would be more effective.
2 Once the students have decided on the way they would like to modify the task, they should write the task description again with the modification included.
3 Ask the students to submit the revised task description together with their work so that your summative comment can take into account the way they changed direction in the course of their writing.

8.8   Satisfying yourself   Level 3↑

Time   25 minutes

Materials   Completed piece of writing

Process stage   Evaluation

Rationale

One thing every writer knows at whatever level they are writing is whether or not they feel pleased with their work. In this activity, the students are given the opportunity to say how they feel about their writing from a subjective point of view, so that you can take this into account when you comment.

Preparation

This activity requires the students to have done a piece of writing which they are due to hand in to you.

Procedure

1 Ask each student to spend two or three minutes deciding how satisfied they are with the piece of writing they are about to hand in.
2 Pair students. Each should tell the other how satisfied they are with their writing and explain why. Partners should help each other to clarify their reasons for how they feel.
3 Ask each student to write a two- or three-sentence comment about the extent to which they are satisfied with their writing at the end of their piece of work and to hand the work and comment in to you. They should indicate what they think is good and less good about their writing.

Variations

i   You can ask the students to list the three best things and one of the poorest things about their writing.
ii   Or to highlight that part of their comment that they would like you to comment on.

iii Or to find a metaphor to express their satisfaction – food, weather, famous people all make good comparisons – so that they might write something like *My writing is like a pizza, crisp on the outside and soft in the middle.*

8.9 Keeping a writer's diary   Level 6↑

Time   20 minutes

Materials   An exercise book or notebook suitable for use as a diary or log

Process stage   Evaluating the development of writing skills

Rationale

The purpose of this activity is to encourage the students to keep writing at the forefront of their thinking over an extended period of time. By keeping a writing diary, they are able to reflect on their progress and develop more acute self-assessment skills. And since they are the principal readers of their own diaries, they are likely to be honest, and even self-critical.

Procedure

On occasions such as when there has been a useful discussion of writing in class, or when you have returned a piece of work, ask the students to write a short diary entry. They can write a comment on their own progress, or on their progress in relation to some aspect of the writing process, or on a particular piece of work, or on the responses they are getting from you, or on how they evaluate their work *vis-à-vis* that of classmates. Encourage them not only to refer to but also to quote from their own work.

Follow-up

You will need to take this diary in from time to time to make sure that it is being kept conscientiously. When you do this, make use of the opportunity to inquire about the extent to which there has been progress since the entry you are commenting on. Try also to make comments which show that you are involved with the way the students are thinking about their own writing. Tip: take in a few diaries each week – it's very difficult to read them all in a single week.

Variations

There are lots of possible variations:

i   Guest entries written by other students who have seen a piece of the diary-keeper's writing.
ii Mother-tongue entries comparing the students' writing skill in the first language with their writing skill in English.
iii An entry written now for the first week of the next term – the students try to predict their writing skill at that stage, etc.

8.10   Completing comment starters   Level 3↑

Time   25 minutes

Process stage   Evaluation

Preparation

1 The students need to have a completed piece of writing to which this activity can be applied.
2 You need to spend a few minutes thinking up sentence starters which are slightly wider in scope than is conventional for comments on writing and are phrased as though spoken by the writer. Some of the following may appeal to you:

> – This piece of writing is good enough to get me a job as ...
> – This piece of writing might satisfy ...
> – My readers will be able to tell that ...
> – I realise that my writing ...
> – The best thing about this piece of writing is ...
> – When I write, I always ...
> – Considering how long I've been learning English ...
> – No one would ...
> – This piece of writing is like ...

Procedure

Dictate each sentence starter at 2–3 minute intervals, thus allowing time for the students to complete each sentence in a way that's true for their piece of writing. Alternatively, write your starters on the board and ask each student to choose the one they would most like to use as a starter to write a paragraph-long comment on their piece of writing. If you dictate starters, you can also dictate two at a time so that the students can choose whichever they feel more comfortable working with.

8.11 Choosing summative comments   Level 5↑

Time   First occasion: 30 plus 5 minutes; each subsequent occasion: 5 minutes

Materials   Completed piece of writing

Process stage   Evaluation

Rationale

In this activity, the students are asked to choose what seem to them to be appropriate objective comments for their own writing. The purpose of this activity is to help the students to take responsibility for the quality of their own work by becoming its judges rather than by leaving it to you to make the judgement.

Preparation

This activity requires the students to have done a piece of writing which they are due to hand in to you.

Procedure

1 The first time you do this activity, you will need to make a list of 15–20 comments which the students might expect to receive on their own writing. A good way to do this is to ask them to look through their exercise books and read out summative comments which they have received for previous work. Adapt any that are too particular so that they make the point in a more general way. Write each comment on the board and ask the students to copy it down. Be ready to add some typical summative comments of your own.

2 After you have made a list on the board and on each subsequent occasion when you use this technique, ask the students to choose two summative comments from the list, the one which they expect you to give them and the one which they hope you might give them. They write these two comments at the end of their piece of writing before handing it in.

Follow-up

When you return the students' work, you will need to comment on the appropriacy of the summative comments chosen by the students for their own work. Do not be afraid to partially agree with one comment only and to make additional comments of your own. It's a good idea to ask the students to work in groups of three and add any new summative comments any of them has received to their existing list. When they next hand work in, they will then have a longer list to choose from.

8.12   Designing an in-writing checklist   Level 5↑

> **Time**   Continuous during writing
>
> **Process stage**   Evaluating while drafting

Rationale

The purpose of this activity is to raise the students' awareness of the need to be constantly evaluating as they write.

Procedure

1 Divide the class into groups of 8 or 10 when you next ask them to do an in-class writing activity. It's important that there is an even number of students in each writing group. Nominate alternate students in each group and explain that you will interrupt the writing after a few minutes and give each of the nominated students a special task. Meanwhile, everyone should get on with the writing task.

2 After the students have been writing for 10–15 minutes, interrupt and explain that each nominated student should write a short reminder to help the other writers in their group. The reminder should be about any item that the other students might have overlooked. It could be something as general as *Check your punctuation now* or as particular as *Use a dictionary to check the first word you have used whose spelling you are unsure of*. The best reminders are often based on something that has already occurred to the reminding writer in the course of this piece of writing – in this way, the students can use their own good ideas to help their colleagues.

3 As soon as a student has written a note, they should pass it to the writer sitting on their left, who acts on it and then passes it to the student sitting on their left, and so on.

Follow-up

You can collect all the notes at the end of the lesson and make an in-writing checklist for use on future occasions. Or merely give out the checklist as a useful set of ideas to keep in mind when writing.

8.13   Picturing the words   Level 4↑

Time   Writing homework, plus 20 minutes

Materials   One picture for each student

Process stage   Evaluating

Rationale

One obvious way of assessing the effectiveness of a piece of writing is for the reader to try and recover the original stimulus. In this activity, each student writes a description of a picture for a reader who then draws the picture which they suppose stimulated the writing.

Preparation

You will need one picture for each student in the class. Pictures of people are best – try to choose relatively simple pictures which show people in rooms or in urban or rural settings. Ideally, you need the same type of picture for each student. Distribute the pictures and ask each student to write as accurate a description of the picture as they can as a homework activity. Set a word limit – 100 words perhaps.

Procedure

1 Ask each student to exchange their writing with a partner, who then tries to draw the picture which stimulated it.
2 When both students have drawn their pictures, pair them and ask them to compare their pictures with the originals. They should work hard at trying to see how the writing would need to be changed to result in drawings more like the originals.

Comment

This is like a picture dictation to the extent that words lead to a picture – the difference is that the words also originated as a picture.

8.14 Getting it right – representing diagrams

Level 4↑

Time 40 minutes

Process stage Evaluating

Preparation

Prepare two different diagrams, each consisting of a circle, a square or rectangle, and an equilateral triangle. These may each be big or small and be placed anywhere on the paper in relation to each other (including within one another or overlapping). Indicate which way up the paper is by writing 'TOP' at the top of the sheet. Copy the following examples if you like. Make copies of one diagram for half the class (one copy per student) and copies of the second diagram for the other half.

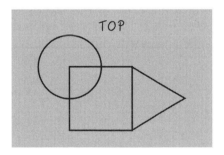 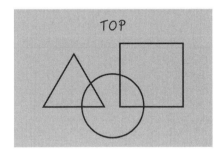

© Cambridge University Press 1998

Procedure

1 Distribute the diagrams and ask each student to write an exact description of what they see in front of them. Make sure that this is not written on the same sheet of paper as the diagram.
2 Collect the diagrams. Explain that you distributed two different diagrams. Ask the students to circulate showing each other their descriptions until they find a partner who has written a description of the other diagram. When they find their partner, they exchange

179

descriptions, return to their places and each student tries to draw the diagram described by their partner.

3 When the diagrams are drawn, ask the students to pair up again and share their results with other pairs, discussing whether the writer or drawer was at fault for any diagrams which went badly wrong.

Follow-up

The students can invent their own diagrams for each other either in class or for homework.

8.15   Responding to drafts   Level 5↑

Time   20 minutes

Materials   First drafts of pieces of writing; post-it notes, preferably in several colours (see *Rationale*)

Process stages   Drafting; rewriting

Rationale

The best time to assess writing in a learning context is at the first draft stage since there is still time for the students to improve it. In this activity, post-it notes (small coloured paper squares with an adhesive rim which allows them to be attached to and removed from other pieces of paper) are used for making suggestions because they don't mess up the draft. For that reason, they are especially useful for peer-assessment when one cannot always rely on the quality of the comments.

Procedure

Ask the students to exchange drafts of their work in progress. Supply one post-it of each colour you have available to each student. If you only have one colour, give each student four post-it notes to start with. Explain that the students are going to make comments on each other's drafts on the post-its and stick them at the most appropriate places on the draft. If you are working with several colours, each colour should be used for a different category of comment. Possible categories include content, spelling, punctuation, accuracy, design/layout, vocabulary, structure. You can specify which categories the students should use, or you can write a list of possible categories on the board and allow them to choose, or you can insist that everyone comments on content and then chooses whichever other categories they think appropriate. Stress that the purpose is to provide the original writers with useful, helpful advice which they can use in a rewrite.

Follow-up

If you wish, you can ask for the drafts and post-its to be handed to you so that you can tick appropriate post-it comments and revise any that are less apt.

8.16   Making the writing fit the comment   Level 3↑

Time   30 minutes

Process stage   Evaluating

Rationale

We know that teachers' comments are often ignored by student writers who cannot see their relevance. Because it's actually very hard indeed to write an accurate comment, one solution is to recognise this by inviting the students to adjust the writing to the comment.

Preparation

The students will need to have completed the final draft of a piece of writing to which this activity can then be applied. Think up a list of one-line positive comments on writing. Some of the following might be possible for intermediate students:

– Your spelling and punctuation are very accurate.
– This is a very good piece of writing indeed. I enjoyed reading it.
– The logical structure of your argument is excellent.
– The quotations from other work contribute a lot to this piece of writing.
– You write very carefully constructed sentences that convey your meaning exactly.
– Your topic is very clearly developed and your conclusion follows logically from this development.
– This piece of work is very well presented.

And some of the following might be possible for elementary students:

- Your spelling and punctuation are very good.
- This is a very good piece of writing indeed.
- Your story is very interesting.
- Your characters talk very naturally.
- Your descriptions are very well written.
- You write simple sentences without error.
- You have taken a lot of trouble planning this piece of writing.
- This piece of work is very well presented.

Procedure

1 Write the prepared list of comments on the board. Ask each student to choose the one they feel comes nearest to being an accurate comment on their piece of writing. It should then be written at the end of the piece of writing followed by the words *except for ...* .
2 Each student should then list any parts of their piece of writing which do not satisfy the positive comment they had written above.
3 If any student wants to adjust their writing before submitting it, give them a last opportunity.

Variation

You can ask the students to exchange their work after Step 1 has been completed so that each student completes Step 2 for their partner's work.

Comment

You can now comment on the comment and on the parts of the writing identified as sub-standard by the author.

8.17 Reading classmates' work Level 4↑

Time   10–15 minutes, plus homework

Materials   Returned pieces of writing with both teacher's comments and a grade

Process stage   Evaluating

Rationale

In the television show *Blind Date* a contestant is asked to choose one of three people whose voices they hear but whom they cannot see. In this activity, the students get to choose a piece of writing to take away and read.

Procedure

1 When you have writing to return to the class with both a comment and a grade on it, group students in fours. Explain that on this occasion and on the next three occasions when you return work, each group of students will play *Blind Date*. One student will be the contestant and will choose one of the pieces of writing produced by the three other students for a 'blind date'.
2 Ask the groups to decide who is the contestant. The other three students read out not their writing, but just your comments on it, both marginal and final. When the contestant has heard them all, they choose which piece of writing to take away and read and, if they want to, to make a further comment of their own on. When the writing has been chosen, the three students all reveal their grades so that the contestant can see how good a choice they made.
3 On each of the next three occasions on which you play *Blind Date*, a different student takes a turn at being the contestant.

Follow-up

If any students don't have their work chosen in the four rounds of *Blind Date* (but see **Comment** below), you can always have them read the most positive comments that you have written on any single piece of their work to the class and then appeal for classmates willing to choose such attractive pieces of writing.

Comment

Although in theory it would be possible for only two of the students in each group of four to have their writing taken away and read, in practice you will find that the groups usually play fair and make sure that each of them has a turn at having their writing chosen.

Bibliography

Brookes, A. and Grundy, P. 1990. *Writing for Study Purposes*. Cambridge: Cambridge University Press.

Brown, P. and Levinson, S.C. 1978/1987. Universals in language usage: politeness phenomena. In E. Goody (ed.) 1978. *Questions and Politeness*. Cambridge: Cambridge University Press 56–311. Reprinted with new introduction and revised bibliography as 1987 *Politeness: Some Universals in Language Usage*. Cambridge: Cambridge University Press.

Flower, L. and Hayes, J. 1981. A cognitive process theory of writing. *College Composition and Communication*, 31, 20–32.

Grabe, W. and Kaplan, R. 1996. *Theory and Practice of Writing*. London: Longman.

Hedge, T. 1988. *Writing*. Oxford: Oxford University Press.

Johns, A. 1990. L1 composition theories: implications for developing theories of L2 composition. In Kroll.

Kroll, B. (ed.) 1990. *Second Language Writing: Research Insights for the Classroom*. Cambridge: Cambridge University Press.

Queneau, R. 1995. *Exercices de Style*. Paris: Gallimard. (Original edition, 1950.)

Raimes, A. 1987. *Exploring through Writing*. New York: St. Martin's Press.

Robinson, P. (ed.) 1988. *Academic Writing: Process and Product*. Modern English Publications and The British Council.

Silva, T. 1990. Second language composition instruction: developments, issues, and directions in ESL. In Kroll.

White, R. 1988. Academic writing: process and product. In Robinson.

Zamel, V. 1983. The composing process of advanced ESL students: Six case studies. *TESOL Quarterly*, 17/2, 165–87.

Indexes

How to use these indexes:

Choose an activity by consulting the five indexes. Then go to the table for your comments which follows. This tells you how the activity you have chosen is organised (pairwork, whole class, etc.) and what stage in the writing process it focuses on. If these are not appropriate to your needs, go back to the indexes and choose another activity.

1 Writing type

2 Topic

3 Working mode

4 Mechanicals

5 Lesson outcomes

Your comments

The table which follows lists all the activities in the book. In the second column, you will find the predominant organisation mode (**Individual, Pairs, Groups, Whole Class**). In the third column, you will find the process stage most focused on (**Planning, Targetting, Organising, Drafting, Evaluating, Editing, Rewriting**). We have also left a space in the table for you to record the date you used the activity, the class you used it with and any comments or improvements you thought of.

Activity	Class organisation	Process Stage	Date used	Class	Comments
1.1	Ind	Ed			
1.2	Ind	Ed			
1.3	Ind	Ed			
1.4	Ind	Org			
1.5	Ind	Ed			
1.6	Ind	Ed			
1.7	Gp	Dra			
1.8	Ind	Re			
1.9	Ind	Re			
1.10	Ind	Dra Re			
1.11	Pr	Dra			
1.12	Gp	Dra			
1.13	Pr	Pl Org Dra			
1.14	Pr	Re			
1.15	I/P	Re			
1.16	Gp	Ev			
2.1	Pr	Ev			
2.2	Gp	Ev			
2.3	Cl	Dra			
2.4	Gp	Ed			
2.5	Gp	Dra			
2.6	Ind	Tar			
2.7	Ind	Ed			
2.8	Gp	Dra			
2.9	Ind	Dra			
3.1	Pr	Pl			
3.2	Cl	Dra			
3.3	Ind	Dra Ev			
3.4	Ind	Pl Dra			
3.5	Gp	Dra			
3.6	Pr	Re			

Activity	Class organisation	Process Stage	Date used	Class	Comments
3.7	Ind	Dra Ed			
3.8	Ind	Ed			
3.9	Pr	Tar Dra			
3.10	Pr	Dra			
3.11	Ind	Org Dra			
4.1	Gp	Pl			
4.2	I/P	Pl Org			
4.3	Gp	Tar			
4.4	Pr	Ta			
4.5	Ind	Org			
4.6	Gp	Pl Org Dra			
4.7	Ind	Tar Org Dra			
4.8	I/P	Re			
4.9	Gr	Re			
4.10	Gp	Re			
5.1	Gp	Pl			
5.2	Gp	Tar			
5.3	Gp	Dra			
5.4	Pr	Dra			
5.5.1	Gp	Org Dra			
5.5.2	Gp	Org Dra			
5.5.3	Gp	Org Dra			
5.6	P/G	Ed Re			
5.7	Gp	Ev			
6.1	IPG	Dra			
6.2	Ind	Dra			
6.3	Ind	Dra Ed			
6.4	Ind	Dra			
6.5	Ind	Ed			
6.6	Ind	Re			
6.7	Ind	Dra			

Activity	Class organisation	Process Stage	Date used	Class	Comments
6.8	I/G	Dra Ed			
6.9	Pr	Pl Dra			
6.10	Ind	Pl			
6.11	I/G	Ed			
6.12	Gp	Pl			
6.13	Gp	Pl Org			
6.14	Gp	Dra			
6.15	Ind	Ev			
6.16	Ind	Ta Or Dr Ev			
7.1	Ind	Dra			
7.2	I/P	Re			
7.3	Gp	Dra			
7.4	I/P	Dra			
7.5	Pr	Pl Dra			
7.6	Ind	Pl Dra			
7.7	Pr	Pl Dra			
7.8	IGP	Org Dra			
7.9	Gr	Or Dr Ev Ed			
7.10	Ind	Pl Org Dra			
7.11	Pr	Dra			
7.12	Gp	Pl Org Dra			
7.13	Pr	Tar Dra Ed			
7.14	Pr	Tar Dra Ev Ed			
7.15	P/C	Pl Org Dra			
7.16	I/P	Dra Ed			
7.17	Pr	Org Dra			
8.1	Cl	Pl Ev			
8.2	Cl	Ev			
8.3	Gp	Pl			
8.4	I/P	Ev			
8.5	I/C	Ev			

Activity	Class organisation	Process Stage	Date used	Class	Comments
8.6	Ind	Ev			
8.7	Ind	Ev			
8.8	Ind	Ev			
8.9	Ind	Ev			
8.10	Ind	Ev			
8.11	Ind	Ev			
8.12	Gp	Ev			
8.13	Pr	Ev			
8.14	Pr	Ev			
8.15	Ind	Re			
8.16	Ind	Dra Ev			
8.17	Gp	Ev			